THE WAY THINGS ARE

A living approach to Buddhism
for today's world

First published by O Books, 2008
Current Version: September 2009
O Books is an imprint of John Hunt Publishing Ltd., The Bothy, Deershot Lodge, Park Lane, Ropley,
Hants, SO24 0BE, UK
office1@o-books.net
www.o-books.net

Distribution in:

UK and Europe
Orca Book Services
orders@orcabookservices.co.uk
Tel: 01202 665432 Fax: 01202 666219
Int. code (44)

USA and Canada
NBN
custserv@nbnbooks.com
Tel: 1 800 462 6420 Fax: 1 800 338 4550

Australia and New Zealand
Brumby Books
sales@brumbybooks.com.au
Tel: 61 3 9761 5535 Fax: 61 3 9761 7095

Far East (offices in Singapore, Thailand,
Hong Kong, Taiwan)
Pansing Distribution Pte Ltd
kemal@pansing.com
Tel: 65 6319 9939 Fax: 65 6462 5761

South Africa
Alternative Books
altbook@peterhyde.co.za
Tel: 021 555 4027 Fax: 021 447 1430

Text copyright: Buddhismus Stiftung
Diamantweg 2008
Design: Stuart Davies & Eveline Smilack
Cover image: Lew Robertson/Getty Images

ISBN: 978 1 84694 042 7

Contributor: Hannah Nydahl
Translator: Kenn Maly
Editors: Eveline Smilack, Claudia Balara
Editor, German Edition: Catrin Hartung
Additional Editors, Glossary: Dafydd Morris, Manfred Seegers

Printed by Digital Book Print

THE WAY THINGS ARE

A living approach to Buddhism
for today's world

Lama Ole Nydahl

BOOKS

Winchester, UK
Washington, USA

CONTENTS

This book is dedicated to all the friends of
Diamond Way Buddhism.

With deepest gratitude to our first lama,
Lama Lopon Tsechu Rinpoche.
He has touched countless beings by his example.

Lama Ole and Hannah Nydahl

**HIS HOLINESS
THE GYALWA KARMAPA**

Dated: The 10th January 2009

This book, which clarifies the Buddha's teachings in an accessible and contemporary format, has proved a popular and useful resource for students of Buddhism since its first publication. This revised and expanded edition will doubtlessly be even more influential in acquainting people with the path to liberation and enlightenment.

Lama Ole Nydahl is one of the closest disciples of my predecessor and a qualified teacher who transmits the flawless teachings of the Karma Kagyu lineage through his activity (Diamond Way). Over the last three decades he has benefited many by presenting the profound timeless methods of the Buddha in a way that is relevant to people in the West.

It is my wish that through this book the seed of Buddhahood is planted in the reader's mind. By putting the teachings presented here into practice, may they accomplish the ultimate goal of enlightenment for the benefit of all.

With best wishes,

**TRINLAY THAYE DORJE
THE 17th GYALWA KARMAPA**

PREFACE

My lovely wife Hannah and I had the exceptionally good fortune to become students of a lama whose every word and action radiated ultimate bliss. From 1969 until 1981, when the 16th Karmapa left his body, we were privileged to be in his close circle and to stay and travel with him in both the East and West. Known as the King of Tibet's yogis, the Karmapa's line of incarnations started in year 1110, was the first in Tibet, and whoever saw him never forgot. Day and night he shared the timeless power of his enlightenment worldwide and with thousands of people. His own living example and the high lamas and accomplishers to whom he sent us transmitted Buddha's ultimate teaching of the Diamond Way methods and the Great Seal (*Mahamudra*) view so powerfully, that even today, his blessing grows with every new generation and continues through his 17th incarnation, Karmapa Trinley Thaye Dorje.

Time is the greatest of gifts. Every new edition of this book has given me the chance to improve it. I am grateful that O-Books had the patience to wait for the translation of this complete revision of *The Way Things Are*, first published by Blue Dolphin in California in 1997. Working with delightful Caty, whose clear overview and untiring dedication structured the latest German edition, a spiritual bestseller that today exists in twenty nine languages. Many thanks to Kenn, who did a wonderful job translating it into English; Claudia and Eve who worked as editors; and all the friends who supported the process.

2007 brought many changes. My wife Hannah became very ill and died in April. The work on this book was very close to her heart and during our last months together, we spent many hours working on it. Her knowledge and inspiring wisdom shine through the pages and were an invaluable contribution. Through our work, we are helping to bring the essence of the accomplisher lineage of Tibetan Buddhism into the modern and approachable form of this book. I would like to share the richness we received and thank our great lineage.

May all beings be free and happy.

Yours, Lama Ole Nydahl
Dakini Day, January 2008, Hamburg.

INTRODUCTION

The buddha of our time, Buddha Shakyamuni, lived 2,450 years ago in the then advanced spiritual culture of Northern India. After his enlightenment, he joyfully taught for a full forty-five years surrounded by highly talented students. Conditions then were ideal for his teachings to be tested and spread widely. This is why his wisdom and methods are also so abundant today. Three important canons of Buddhist teachings developed: the Tibetan canon (*Kangyur/Tengyur*), the Chinese canon, and the Pali canon. The Kangyur consists of 108 volumes and contains 84,000 different teachings. They are Buddha's own words, written down after his death by students with precise memories. The Tengyur is an additional 254 volumes with clarifications of Buddha's words by his experienced students. Both the Kangyur and the Tengyur were translated into Tibetan between the seventh and fourteenth centuries.

Leaving his body at the age of eighty, Buddha said, "I can die happily. I have not kept a single teaching hidden in a closed hand. Everything that is useful for you, I have already given. Be your own guiding light." Such statements show that his teachings focus on human maturity and real life. When asked why and what he taught, Buddha's answer was just as direct, "I teach because you and all beings want to have happiness and want to avoid suffering. I teach *the way things are.*"

Many schools evolved out of the vastness of these teachings, all aiming to align beings' body, speech, and mind with Buddha's. They develop human potential by using layered practices that he recommended. Since his teachings are all encompassing in scope and build on experience and not belief, it does not suffice to simply list their contents. Only in comparison with other worldviews and religions does Buddha's unique contribution become clear. It is also advisable to approach the subject matter with a minimum of fixed ideas.

Many people in the West may see Buddhism as a form of philosophy. This is true to the degree that Buddha's teachings are completely logical. Clarity and freedom of thought are functions of well developed minds and constantly increase in strength as one approaches that state. If the teachings cause beings' abilities, predominantly the logical, to fully blossom, why not call Buddhism a philosophy?

Philosophy works on the level of concepts. One takes pleasure in a perfect argument and then puts the book back on the shelf. Buddha's teachings, however, go beyond concepts. They produce a practical and lasting transformation of body, speech, and mind. Making people aware of the daily functioning of their minds, as well as supplying a beyond personal view of the outer world, Buddha's teachings deeply transform those practicing them.

Even in the first stages of practice, applying a Buddhist understanding and Buddha's liberating methods to one's life will dissolve any feeling of being a helpless victim. Confidence then emerges as one sees that events follow a pattern of cause and affect and can therefore be controlled, which again sharpens one's appetite for further knowledge. With such increased awareness, one acts ever more effortlessly and beneficially from an unshakeable center. Because Buddha's teachings fundamentally change whoever practices them, Buddhism is more than a philosophy.

Others may wonder if Buddhism is psychology. Buddhist practitioners who are properly instructed frequently report tangible results even after a short exposure, such as increased calmness, satisfaction, and inner strength. Some may therefore claim that Buddhist teachings are really a kind of psychology. What can be said about that? The goal of this fine science is clear: to improve people's daily lives. All schools of psychology wish for society to get some use out of each individual, so that no one suffers or burdens others too much over the seventy to ninety years that most live in Western countries today.

Insofar as Buddha's teachings bring about the same results, psychology and Buddhism do share these same relative goals. But

Buddha's teachings go much further: they show that no conditioned mental state is permanent, that ultimately nothing transient can be trusted. For those willing to trust the mirror behind the images and the ocean beneath the waves, Buddhism points out what is between and behind the thoughts, establishing the experience of timeless awareness itself. Only this realization elucidates the qualities that can carry beings through old age, sickness, loss, and even death.

In principle, Buddha took his "psychology" beyond the experienced flow of causality during this lifetime. He proved that the ultimate essence of mind shared by all beings is empty of any quality that might limit it in time and space. By example, he demonstrated beyond any doubt that the flow of physical and mental experiences that people identify with, and consider themselves to be, is fundamentally impermanent and unreal. He explained that the conditioned relative mind that beings experience is a stream of changing impressions held together by the illusion of a self. This illusory self, in conjunction with others, creates the world and every being's experience of it since beginningless time. He taught that events and experiences, whose origins are not comprehensible in terms of this life, must stem from actions during former existences. Correspondingly, one's thoughts, words, and actions today, if not transformed or purified, will determine the future into which one will be born. This all pervading principle of cause and effect is called *karma* and explains why beings' outer and inner circumstances are so varied.

The realization that beings experience the outcome of their own thoughts, words, and actions makes way and goal clear; and one's activity can start at a mature level of self-confidence and independence. This knowledge is not easy for everyone to accept, especially not for people who find themselves in difficult situations. Buddha, however, avoided any moralistic finger pointing and taught that the cause of suffering is not evil, but fundamental ignorance, that keeps beings from seeing themselves as part of a totality. Removing this ignorance removes negativity and thereby leads to lasting happiness, which is everyone's goal.

Both psychology and Buddhism thus change people. While psychology remains in the everyday conditioned realm however, Buddhism transcends all experienced dualities by showing mind's essence to be timeless and uncreated. Proving both the outer and inner worlds to be transient and empty of any lasting essence, one may blissfully relax in both. The teachings point to the experiencer and the richness of perceiving mind. Buddha inspires people to realize that life's goal cannot be a comfortable and blank existence until its end, but rather must be the constantly growing challenge of discovering one's full potential.

When does the inclination arise to consciously direct one's life? Once people understand the law of cause and effect and seek tools to actively escape their own pain, when they have stored so many good impressions that it would be constricting not to share them with others, and when they discover the unlimited potential of beings and situations, and understand that living fully is highest bliss. To be successful in such endeavors it helps to first observe that little can be done for others as long as one's own feelings, words, and actions are harmful. Then we recognize the satisfaction of having compassion and thinking clearly on a beyond personal level. Finally, some people are instantly inspired by living examples who convincingly mirror mind's open, able, and unlimited essence. They simply cannot wait to become like these teachers.

Whatever reasons motivate one and on whichever level one wants to enter the practice, Buddhist methods bring courage, joy, power, and the richness of love. They allow one's potential of body, speech, and mind to continually increase. With a growing awareness that everything is constantly changing, one finds freedom. The realization that nothing in the conditioned realm lasts or truly exists, that birth and death apply to all, that peoples' wish for happiness and attempts to avoid pain are similar everywhere, that beings are countless while one is only singular, gradually leads to perceptions beyond the personal. All disturbing feelings become rootless when the non-existence of a solid or lasting *self* or *I* in body or mind is recognized. Thus a first step is realized, which is not a goal in itself but a gift on the way to benefiting all: the state of liberation. Here, the illusion of a separate ego is dissolved and one no longer identifies with suffering. This is the foundation for the ultimate stage of all knowing enlightenment.

The second and final step in one's development, enlightenment is mind's full realization, the effortless and fully conscious resting in the *here and now*. This self-arisen intuitive state appears with the dissolution of all limiting concepts. When habitual *either / or* thinking loosens its stranglehold and space emerges for a wider view of *both / and*, countless capacities inherent in mind are awakened. Many know the taste of this from striking and explosively happy moments in life. Suddenly all is meaningful and one is united with everything. Space then no longer separates, but rather holds everything as a potential and a container. It gives meaning to all, conveys and embraces everything. With enlightenment, mind's power of perception becomes unlimited, much clearer, and more exciting than anything conceptualized or known. As the experience of bliss and inspiration never fades, it would be an unusual result to discuss in a session with one's psychologist.

There is a third view, which claims that Buddhism is a religion, although it is different from what Western societies normally understand when they talk about religion. One fundamental difference appears when examining the word itself. The meaning of the Latin prefix *re-* means back or again and *ligare* meaning to bind or unite. It expresses how the Middle Eastern faith religions, that have dominated much of the world for a thousand years, essentially try to find their way back to something perfect. Religions of experience, however, such as Buddhism, could hardly trust a re-established state, a paradise out of which one had already fallen, to be solid. That would mean that this state was not originally absolute and could be lost again at any time.

From a Buddhist viewpoint, we have always been confused because mind, being like an eye, cannot see itself. As Buddha's teachings are a mirror that enables mind to recognize its inherent aware and timeless essence and know itself as encompassing subject, object and action, once found this understanding is never lost again.

If one takes Buddhism to be a religion, one must distinguish between various kinds of convictions. There are the religions of faith that intervene heavily in the lives of human beings, like Judaism, Christianity, and above all Islam, (literally meaning submission, which prescribes every action to be either done or avoided and completely lacks natural morality.) Their gods exhibit exceedingly personal and frequently disturbing human character-istics, which Christianity and Judaism have declared historical but are irrelevant in today's world. In contrast to these religions are the Far Eastern non-dogmatic religions of experience, like the crown of Hinduism called *Advaita-Vedanta*, much of Taoism, and Buddhism. Their goal is the realization of mind's potential.

As mentioned, these two types of religions have fundamentally different goals and methods. The religions of faith that are so dominant in the world today, all arose in a small area of the Middle East. Their political focus is historically the city of Jerusalem and their common root is the Old Testament, which found its current form in their tribal societies a few thousand years ago.

The societies of the Middle East were then, and still are today, occupied with the continual battle for dominance and survival. That is why they worship male gods, compete for followers, and hold everything together with laws given by gods. Founded on such conditions the idea of a creating, punishing, and judging outer force was forged, a power whose truth had to be separate from that of human beings. Because such a claim is essentially not testable or achievable, it must simply be believed. The task of the unreformed and submissive believer is thus fulfilling the wishes of such outer forces and their representatives, who proselytized teachings consisting of dogmas, prohibitions, and commands. Believers must also cling to a conviction that is contrary to a mature experience, namely that one path alone is true and good for everyone and all other ways are bad. Over the last 2,000 years, religions have probably killed more people than politics and in less humane ways. Any civilized society should consider them a dangerous luxury and seriously monitor their behavior.

Arising in Northern India and China at about the same time as the Old Testament, the Far Eastern religions of experience exerted much less pressure. Their richer and more civilized societies were probably less peaceful and more brutal than many today want to believe, but their wars were not religious. There were people with similar views in every army and their goals were worldly. They were surely rich cultures with abundance. Many philosophical directions existed at the same time, and many people had a pervading wish for information and freedom of mind. Under such conditions, religions developed an entirely different orientation; their goal became a better life for people, the unfolding of their human potential. One finds little inclination among them towards the regulations that force everyone's views into one direction. Even when fighting for money, land, or influence, the various and practical approaches to truth were seen as useful for people's different private situations. For example, Buddha constantly warned his students against simply believing his teachings. Instead he wanted all who came to ask questions and to test and confirm his words through their own experience. His wish for everyone was and is today, the spiritual freedom empowering one to reach enlightenment.

For this, a step-by-step method is useful for most, until an unshakeable foundation of good karma, compassion, wisdom, and beyond personal awareness is developed. From that point on, results appear naturally because one realizes that the fulfilment one has been searching for has always existed inside oneself. It is simply one's mind.

Knowing this, Buddha trusted the independence, talents, and abilities of his students as means to their fulfilment. Holding before them the liberating and enlightening mirror of his teachings, he showed them what riches lie hidden in everyone. Therefore beings' potential for enlightenment is called *buddha nature*. Without confidence in this beyond personal state there is neither way nor goal.

This view of inherent perfection is Buddhism's fundamental difference from the world's faith based religions. Hinduism and Taoism both include some absolute teachings similar to or inspired by Buddhism. This was a natural result in these societies with such tribal closeness inside India and Tibet. But neither of these traditions absorbed them fully.

Buddha avoided what today is called *esoteric*. Although it is touching how some people have tried to keep the idealistic feeling of the 1960's alive without drugs through the chrome-plated egotism of the following decades, their purely emotive approach to understanding the world is not enough. To clearly know mind, one has to perfect all aspects of oneself, including critical reasoning. Mixing together pleasant sounding spiritual fragments from various sources and marketing these as timeless truths brings only sweet confusion. Even with the finest of new packaging, but without the confirmation of generations of real experience, such mixing does not move beyond the realm of concepts and words. Real knowledge always moves beyond and has massive power.

So what does Buddha teach as ultimately true? He explains that a timeless essence pervades, knows, and is the foundation of everything. That something absolute must be always and everywhere, never created nor destroyed; otherwise it would be conditioned and relative. Space and its richness of potential pervade beyond the concepts of what is and what is not. By creating the right conditions, one can realize such blissful truth. The inability to experience all or parts of this, until enlightenment, comes from the fundamental fault of any unenlightened mind: its inability to know itself.

All of Buddha's teachings are directed to mind's nature and give ways to bring about its full awakening. If one searches for any timeless and indestructible consciousness looking through one's eyes, being aware of or experiencing things, one finds nothing solid, existent, or factual. That is why Buddha explains mind's essence as being *empty*. The understanding in his time would be *empty of something*, thus the word was useful to express that the awareness being investigated has no substance or definite properties. With that term, people would then not associate emptiness with a nothingness or a black hole. They would rather understand that the experiencer has neither size nor weight, neither depth, width, nor length, that mind is not a thing that can ever fall apart or disappear.

A mathematician today would probably designate mind's essence as the neutral element of things. A scientist would talk of inherent potential, and a craftsman could say, "It is not a thing." A lover or a warrior, who experiences the world as an extension of one's senses, would experience mind as open space.

This pointing to mind's empty essence conveys deep confidence. Although bodies die and thoughts come and go, that which experiences is neither born nor made. Therefore mind remains beyond death, decay, or dissolution. In essence it is like space: a timeless container that lets everything appear; it embraces, knows, and connects all phenomena. There is also no external force in which one must believe. Each person is responsible for his or her own situation and development. Through his example, Buddha embodies an ultimate goal that everyone can reach. By knowing one's essence better through his teachings, one obtains a genuine refuge and steady support is provided on a daily level, from the beginning of one's way until enlightenment.

In Indochina, excluding Vietnam, and in Sri Lanka, a reasonable goal to Buddhist practice is seen in the state called *liberation*. This means the removal of the illusion of being a lasting and individual *me*. On the other hand, the Northern schools of Buddhism aim for full *enlightenment*, the full removal of any dualistic ideas. Especially for the latter and ultimate goal, one needs Buddha's highly philosophical and psychological teachings: the so-called Great Way and especially the tools of the Diamond Way. Here the importance of the guru, or lama, one's trusted friend while developing, increases in tandem with effectiveness.

Buddha's teachings are the key to lasting happiness. Through this knowledge, he appears as one's teacher, protector, and friend. Using his advice one may avoid suffering, develop oneself in a powerful way, and help others. Buddha himself chose the name that best describes his teachings: *Dharma* in Sanskrit and *Cheu* in Tibetan. In the West, this term translates as *the way things are*.

BUDDHA'S LIFE AND TEACHINGS

BUDDHA'S LIFE STORY

Birth and Youth at Court

An overview of Buddha's life makes his teachings relevant today. Approximately 2,450 years ago, he was born into a royal family in Northern India. Several centuries earlier, during one of several mass migrations, his ancestors from the Shakya clan colonized the area, coming from what is today Ukraine and central Russia. The Buddha belonged to the Warrior caste and the texts describe him as tall and very strong. His parents' kingdom lay at the southern border of what is today Nepal, near Lumbini in the region called Kapilavastu. The area at that time was rich and not overpopulated. Excavations show that there was an underground sewage system, as well as central heating between the double walls of some houses, meaning that local culture was well developed at that time. Buddha himself was certainly no virgin birth. He was the very last chance for his parents to have a child and thus a successor to the throne.

At an age when she had already given up hope, his mother had a powerful dream announcing her pregnancy. Standing in a grove fifteen miles from the palace, she gave birth to a strong and beautiful boy. His parents were ecstatic. They gave him the name Siddhartha Gautama and expected him to become a powerful king. Without a strong general at their helm, kingdoms at that time quickly disappeared.

Gradually however, his parents noticed signs that hinted at something different. Wherever the boy went, flowers appeared. "Is he a poet, a dreamer, a philosopher?" they asked. To find out, his parents invited three meditators to predict their son's future. After thoroughly examining him, all said the same thing, "The boy is truly special. If he is kept from the pain and dissatisfaction of the world, he will accomplish your every wish. A perfect warrior and hero, he will conquer all neighboring kings and you will be proud of him. If however, he discovers that the world is conditioned and cannot bring any lasting happiness, he will renounce everything. He will develop a new and enlightening view and bring this into the world."

Since they wanted a ruler and not an artist or a dropout, Buddha's parents acted quickly. They surrounded the growing prince with everything a healthy young man likes: five hundred select women, opportunities for sports, excitement, and above all, the important combat training that he completely mastered. They also provided the best conditions for his intellectual training and in this too he soon excelled. His every wish was met and for the first twenty nine years of his life, he experienced only shifting aspects of joy. As his store consciousness contained nothing disturbing from former lives, there were no unpleasant impressions from within that could surface. Everything that was potentially painful had been kept from the young prince. Then suddenly, his world turned upside down.

Disillusionment and Search for Meaning

Leaving his castle on three successive days at the age of twenty nine, he met with suffering in its most immediate aspects. He saw someone desperately sick, someone wrecked with age, and finally someone dead. Returning to his palace, young Prince Siddhartha had a terrible night. He was beyond thinking of himself, but the awareness that pain strikes everyone gave him no rest. Wherever he looked, he found nothing that he could offer his dear ones as a refuge from it. There was nothing that could be relied upon. Fame, family, friends, and possessions, everything would go away. He discovered only impermanence. Nothing was real or lasting in the external or internal world.

The next morning, feeling like a question mark with his mind wrapped up in this dilemma, the prince walked past a meditator who sat in deep absorption. When their eyes met and their minds linked, Siddhartha stopped, mesmerized. This man might be showing him what he was looking for, a true and real refuge. His state displayed a mirror behind the images, an ocean underneath the waves, mind's eternal awareness through all its appearing, changing, and dissolving images. The future Buddha had a sudden insight that there might be something unchanging and conscious between and behind all ideas and impressions.

"This must be it!" he thought. Trusting the experiencer but not the changing experiences seemed utterly reasonable. Meeting that man gave the future Buddha a first and enticing taste of mind, which he knew he had to experience himself for the good of all. In a flash, he realized that the perfection he had been seeking outside must be within mind itself.

At that time there were no tools or teachings for using an exciting life to ride the tiger of direct experience to enlightenment. So the prince decided to renounce his rich but distracting private life in order to limit the number of disturbing impressions reaching his mind. He fled his palace during the night and disappeared into the clearings and woods of Northern India. He had to realize the mightiest of goals: mind's timeless essence.

Passionately wanting to know mind fully and inspired by all beings' wish for lasting happiness, no exercise was too difficult or unpleasant for the future Buddha. The following six years were hard, but he matured in every aspect. Wherever he went, he learned without fear or pride. When he was fed the dualistic teaching that the body is bad, he first fasted himself down to nearly a skeleton. But when he discovered that his physical weakness confused him rather than strengthening his clarity of mind, making it impossible to help others or himself, he began eating again and quickly regained his strength.

All of today's known schools of thought were already present in Northern India at that time, and Siddhartha learned from the most eminent teachers of them all. Soon outpacing them, he was disappointed that they all showed him mind's potential but not mind itself. Their dualistic explanations brought him no closer to his goal. Knowing nothing of any experiencer, they could not confirm anything lasting in which he could put his trust. He therefore thanked them and took his leave.

In all non-Buddhist cultures, even the most highly gifted teachers imagined gods and other unprovable causes for the world and its events. Among them only Buddha, and his great contemporary Heraclitus in Greece, came to the unique, logical, and conclusive view that space is in itself pregnant and brings forth all outer and inner worlds: that it is joyfully at play and that all possibilities reside within it.

Conditions in Northern India 2,450 Years Ago

An unusual spiritual openness reigned in India at Buddha's time, similar to that in ancient Greece, the Italian Renaissance, and the 1960's in the West. In comparison to the freedoms enjoyed today, in part because of modern hygiene and methods of birth control, life at Buddha's time was more prudish. With regard to the depth of their motivation and the clarity of their philosophy of life, however, many of his students were more aware and much less distracted than people are today. The dominant viewpoints of materialism, nihilism, existentialism, and transcendentalism were as prevalent then as they are now. Above all, however, the Indians of that time expected spirituality to influence their daily lives in positive ways and they were much less spoiled.

In Buddha's time people were not yet stigmatized by absolutism or totalitarian religions. They expected more from a worldview than the wishes of personal gods who gave dogmas of faith but still had self declared imperfections like jealousy, pride, and anger. For people then to accept a philosophy of life, it had to go beyond anything personal and provide access to timeless truth. The teachings had to have a logical basis, possess useable methods, and demonstrate a reachable goal. At the same time, claims to truth were dealt with very responsibly. If during a public debate, someone advocated a point of view that someone else could refute, the loser was expected to become the winner's student. Intellectual honesty demanded it.

Enlightenment

During his six years of learning and meditating in the then forested and pleasant plains of Northern India, the young prince's promises from countless past lives matured. He only wanted to recognize mind's essence and bring the greatest of gifts to all. To achieve this, he chose a seat near a stream in a place now called Bodhgaya.

Today Bodhgaya is a village of many Buddhist temples, situated two–thirds of the way from Delhi to Calcutta. The nearest town, Gaya, lies in the now hopelessly overpopulated state of Bihar. Despite tourists, beggars, and the usual Indian confusion, the site still possesses an immense power field. Over recent years, the region around the vast Buddhist stupa and the village has become quite dangerous. The holy places, like the caves of the six-armed protector to the right of the road to Gaya, can only be visited during the day, in large groups, and with weapons. People are killed there by the villagers, sometimes merely for their clothes.

At Bodhgaya, sitting down under a spread out leafy tree near a brook, the future Buddha decided to remain in meditation until he knew mind and could benefit all beings. After spending six rich and eventful days and nights cutting through mind's most subtle obstacles, he reached enlightenment on the full moon morning of May, approximately 2,425 years ago, a week before he turned thirty five. As is known, he died on that same day forty five years later. At the moment of full realization, all veils of mixed feelings and stiff ideas dissolved and Buddha experienced the all encompassing here and now. All separation in time or space disappeared. Past, present, and future, near and far, melted into one radiant state of intuitive bliss. Thus he became timeless, all pervading awareness. Through every cell in his body he knew and was everything.

For the first seven weeks after his enlightenment, the newly Awakened One, the fourth of a thousand buddhas to manifest while there is intelligent life on earth, remained under his tree in Bodhgaya. He needed to get his body accustomed to the intense streams of energy now filling it. Here, the main Hindu gods like Mahadeva and Brahma came to Buddha and requested him to teach, received instructions and took refuge, which some of them still remember and others forgot. Like the brightest people that came later, many gods did not experience Buddha as a man, a god, or something outer, but rather as a mirror to their own essential nature. His example showed them truly reliable values.

Refuge

Throughout his years of teaching, the Buddha advised his students to rely on the Three Jewels, also called the Three Rare and Precious Ones. This is done formally by opening oneself to Buddha, Dharma, and Sangha. This outer refuge is common to all Buddhist schools and is a necessary condition for coming to know mind. Whether this refuge is explained in great detail or if one simply repeats a few sentences after the teacher, a bond between mind's unrecognized inner potential and the objects of refuge develops. From then on, using Buddha's methods, one's confidence will grow knowing that mind contains enlightened qualities and that they may actually one day be discovered.

The first refuge is in Buddha as the goal. He represents mind's full realization and embodies enlightenment with its qualities of highest wisdom, compassion, view, and strength. This state, known as buddha nature, pervades space and dwells in all beings as mind's indestructible and timeless Truth Essence, even if one is not aware of it. The second refuge consists of his teachings, the Dharma, his 84,000 enlightening instructions. When opening up to Buddha's teachings as the way to enlightenment, one will naturally seek the company of others with similar values. The third refuge is Sangha, friends on the way. They are the group of people with whom we develop in our Buddhist practice. Surrounding oneself as much as possible with advanced people, and sharing similar values is important on the way. Developing together with close friends is simply the best.

Buddha is the main refuge for the Buddhist schools that focus on transmission and meditation. Through his inspiring example, one gets an inkling of mind's absolute state in which nothing changes. Above all, the experience of one's own teacher should help one trust this inherent essence. The Buddhist schools that rely more on intellectual analysis and debate, stress the teachings of the Dharma as the main refuge. This is because they bring one to a buddha state. In this case, perfection is reached more slowly, step-by-step, but in a level headed way.

As one's access to a skillful role model increases and one's practice becomes more total, the significance of the Sangha increases and their conscious way of living becomes a teaching in itself. They remain as one's friends but are now seen as bodhisattvas, as people striving for enlightenment. By placing others' spiritual growth above their own, bodhisattvas quickly master both the conditioned world and their own mind.

Here one may distinguish two types of practitioners. The realized ones are unshakeable and fearless. They understand the non-existence of any ego or self, that mind is space and cannot be hurt. These are the people that one can completely rely upon. Their example expertly leads others from confusion to enlightenment. Also one's more usual companions are important. Those who are still developing their yo-yo minds through the minefields of powerful emotions share one's motivation of reaching enlightenment for the benefit of all. If they are willing to not take things personally, they will interact openly with others. Thus all learn from the phases that each one in the group passes through.

The goal (Buddha), the way (Dharma), and one's friends (Sangha) are essential to all schools of Buddhism and provide ten to fifteen percent of the world's population with advice and protection towards a meaningful and independent life. The schools focusing on the inner practices and deeper philosophy also take a fourth refuge, in the teacher or *guru*. In Sanskrit guru means heavy (with good qualities) and *lama*, in Tibetan, means highest principle. For the methods of the Diamond Way, the teacher is the most important refuge. He represents the ultimate level of identifying with enlightenment. These teachings were transmitted by the old, or Red Hat schools in Tibet, and in some Japanese Zen and Chinese Chan Buddhist traditions as well. The lama in these schools guarantees proven and direct access to the space and bliss of enlightenment. As an example to others, he should balance beyond personal wisdom with active love for all beings.

On the Diamond Way level, along with giving the outer refuge of the Three Jewels (Buddha, Dharma and Sangha), the teacher also represents and transmits the Three Roots of quick and total growth and the blessing of his spiritual lineage. His methods (Tibetan: *Yidam*) and initiations unite mind with its absolute nature. His protector energies bring strength and activity and transform every experience into a step towards enlightenment.

In the Diamond Way, the lama is the practical embodiment of the whole refuge. The more skillful the methods are, the more important the teacher becomes. Everyone manages to learn how to walk by themselves. When learning to drive, instructions are useful to most. However, nobody will successfully learn how to fly without a teacher.

Nothing is more important than the values by which one orients one's life. Thus from the earliest possible moment, Buddha's students convey one basic truth: Phenomena come and go and only mind is a lasting refuge. Recognizing its space is highest bliss.

THE THREE WAYS

The Small Way — The Four Noble Truths

Seven weeks after his enlightenment, Buddha taught humans for the first time in a Deer Park near Sarnath, a town seven miles from Benares, today known as Varanasi. It is most holy to Hindus, who burn their dead there and entrust the remains to the Ganges River. A successful pilgrimage to the site includes bathing in the river and drinking its delicious water.

Five seekers came to him there, true moralists. They had become holy in the wrong sense of the word, not whole and full of energy, but stiff and joyless instead. They were the kind of customers that any teacher, wishing a healthy development in his groups, would surely send elsewhere. They thought only of themselves, judged others, and aimed solely to get rid of their own suffering. Before Buddha's enlightenment, when he nearly fasted himself to death, they had been quite impressed. However, when Buddha discovered this approach to be useless and resolved to restore his health, they considered him too worldly and left him.

Coming upon him at the Deer Park in Sarnath, they were disturbed by his joy and effortless radiance. First they tried to ignore him, but as his power-field enveloped them, they had no choice but to pay attention and asked, "Why do you shine? How did you get this way?" In answer to these seekers Buddha gave the Four Noble Truths: Conditioned existence is suffering. This suffering has a cause. It has an end. There are ways leading to that end.

The many Buddhist schools that have come and gone over the last 2,450 years have offered quite different interpretations of these statements, but their general meaning is common. Even though they were originally taught to listeners motivated by reaching their own liberation, Buddha's words touch all levels of understanding and their usefulness increases with one's level of insight. Realized from the ultimate view, that highest functioning is highest bliss, the Four

Noble Truths supply a very useful frame for all of Buddha's teachings.

These four sentences are pointed and were Buddha's first known words to human students, given to people most aware of suffering but not of joy. There are still some consequences for living Buddhism even today. Although all images, statues, and pictures show Buddhas smiling, due to these statements, many educated people expect Buddhism to basically be a teaching of logical pessimism.

The holders of Buddha's transmission today must therefore frequently fight against life negating interpretations of his words to keep the way free for happy people to enter the teachings. For instance, this gloomy view regularly appears when people come across the term *Nirvana*, which has two aspects: the accomplishment of either a secure mental peace or enlightenment, which translates as *blowing it out*. The initial interpretation at our universities was that Buddhists want to fall into nothingness or a black hole after death. However this view expresses a superficial understanding. If Nirvana was to denote a simple disappearance, the experience of consciousness itself as timeless limitless bliss in meditation would not be attainable. Therefore it is most important not to translate terms expressing absolute mental states using dualistic concepts like the habitual division of good or bad, being or not being, but to use all mind's aspects and perceive through the total view of both/and.

The first Noble Truth, "There is suffering," elicits the natural responses, "What kind of defeatist view is that?" or, "To whom does he hope to sell such a bad trip?" More dramatic religions arrive on the scene with more impressive style by exclaiming, "My God is the only one," or, "My God is the strongest," or, "Allah's revenge is merciless and unfailing." Such religions provide certainty to the weak, give the illusion of removing personal responsibility, which is not possible, and supply a feeling of being part of a powerful whole.

Seen from a more mature perspective, however, a deeper meaning emerges from this first Noble Truth: The basis of Buddha's teachings is boundless happiness. How is this to be understood? Almost everyone forgets the conditioned nature of outer and inner phenomena and that above all else, experiences are dependent on the nature of the experiencer. Surely no Buddha is needed to tell people that they have better and worse days. Even with most practicing Buddhists, such fluctuations cease only after many years of practice.

All beings seem to be conscious of how they feel, a capacity that seems to be independent of whatever other talent they may possess. On this point, no help is needed. Buddha only becomes necessary for pointing out what people usually do not comprehend. Without him, they miss the radiant mirror behind the images, the timeless and unconditioned consciousness behind all things, the experience of highest bliss inherent in mind's richness, the joy that encompasses everything and is inseparable from enlightenment.

"There is suffering," thus carries the ultimate meaning that, compared to the experience of timeless awareness, even the best experience is pale and may therefore be described as suffering. It expresses Buddha's insight that every changing event is secondary to mind's timeless radiance, which so few realize. Next to the spontaneous power of conscious space, even the most precious moments of excitement and love are mere shadows of one's true essence. The most beautiful of waves is less fulfilling than the depth of the ocean itself.

Therefore Buddha's first Noble Truth is not as pessimistic as it might appear to some. Rather, it is immensely uplifting. Whoever shows the nature of timeless mind to be more perfect than all of its fleeting games makes all rich beyond bounds.

Buddha's second Noble Truth is, "Suffering has a cause." Hearing this, the seekers in the Deer Park must have wondered which cause he meant. Here, Buddha pointed to only one culprit: the basic ignorance of any unenlightened mind. It influences body and speech and keeps everyone from the happiness they seek. Because the untrained mind is unable to perceive that the seer, the objects seen, and the act of seeing itself interact, condition one another, and are aspects of the same totality, an experience of separation arises. The meaning of all Buddha's teachings and the goal of every Buddhist meditation is only to dissolve one's entrapment in this illusion.

Cutting the knot of ignorance, however, is not so easy. Up to the moment of enlightenment, consciousness mainly functions like an eye. It notices outer and inner events but experiences itself only accidentally and then only in brief but overwhelming moments. Such breakthrough situations will only become stable in meditators, because so many things distract untrained minds. They evaluate the emotional resonance of every situation and qualities of every object and take the most transient of thoughts and feelings very seriously.

Few, however, perceive the experiencer. Countless lives are spent chasing impermanent and constantly changing appearances, missing out on the timeless bliss that is mind's essence. This beginningless and ongoing inability to recognize mind as the foundation of any world or experience is the cause of all suffering.

Due to this, the ongoing stream of sensual and emotional impressions is perceived as an *I*. What is experienced, that which this space brings forth, then becomes a *you* and the external world. Although by their very nature all phenomena appear, change constantly, and exist only as flowing and conditioned states, one still believes transitory appearances to be real and separate from mind. In Buddha's teachings, this most grievous mistake is called basic ignorance. It is the cause of all pain and disturbing situations anywhere.

The mistaken feeling of separation between an illusory *me* and an equally unreal *you*, between a here and a there, naturally brings about two very unpleasant emotions: attachment, the attempt to attain what is pleasant, and aversion, the attempt to avoid one's dislikes and what is unpleasant. Such ugly parents beget equally ugly offspring. From attachment arises greed, the wish to store and hold onto what one likes, while aversion causes envy, disliking the happiness of others. Finally, ignorance leads to exclusive pride, which brings absolutely no satisfaction. Competing with others on the slippery stage of fame, youth, wealth, or beauty, one can only lose, wasting time and making life exceedingly constricted and poor. Feeling better than others, one is by definition always in bad company. Then spontaneously sharing whatever joys may still appear is difficult because one must constantly check who is now better or worse. Inclusive pride on the other hand, basking in the fine qualities of others and thinking, "Aren't we all great?" brings lasting happiness.

As long as basic ignorance persists, these six disturbing emotions are inevitable. Worse than that, they may manifest in up to 84,000 combinations of mental veils. Although such feelings have no lasting essence and change constantly, those who do not meditate will believe them to be real. The untrained mind is unable to recognize that these emotions were not there earlier, will not be there later, and that it would be foolish to give them energy now. Instead, most people jump right into any drama and surrender reason, speech, and body to whatever strong emotion appears. As one may expect, this sows further seeds of pain and confusion in one's own subconscious and in the world, leading to future trouble.

This negative causality is only broken once people start acting consciously, with altruism, kindness, and understanding for others. Like a doctor, who from compassion may inflict a lesser pain to avoid a bigger one, motivation is king. With a positive wish, even powerful acts, disturbing some but bringing freedom to many, will be noble.

A fearless mind and a desire to help others will strengthen one's character and future usefulness to the world. However, if residual negative feelings have become involved, or an ignoble motivation is suddenly noticed, it is wise to stick one's hands deeply into one's pockets and leave them there or to fill one's mouth with chewing gum instead of speaking.

Although obstacles are ultimately brought about by a person's own disturbing feelings, clumsy words, or harmful actions in this or former lives, almost everyone imagines that others are at fault. It is too easily overlooked that all beings create their own karma and world. This circle of mixed and misunderstood causes and effects, called *Samsara* in Sanskrit and *Khorwa* in Tibetan, imprisons all who do not recognize the timeless awareness behind the events. It is the wheel of conditioned and limited existence.

Faith religions are not particularly convincing on this subject. They believe that personal and good or at least so-called righteous gods are absolute forces that create the world. They must therefore include and insist on equally improvable negative forces as the causes of the trouble and pain that they cannot deny. Though this dualistic thinking has added much drama, excitement, pain, and suppression to history, it is illogical from any philosophical point of view. As action and reaction evidently work, and any energy expressed returns to its cause, something totally evil would constantly self destruct.

In the religions of experience, however, and above all in Buddhism, every being is responsible for oneself. The teachings contain no moral pressure from the outside, only advice or help to consciously do one's best. They are based on the observation that all beings have buddha nature and want happiness. Harmful deeds and their unpleasant consequences therefore emerge from ignorance and a lack of maturity, rather than from an informed choice or inherent evil. They may be removed and even transformed into insight before they mature into pain. The Dharma offers the views and methods to control, eliminate or even transform the causes of any upcoming problem. For example, Buddha advises strongly against revenge. Instead, one should forgive people to cut any bonds and avoid having to see their unpleasant faces next life again

Since karma is the natural unfolding of cause and effect, and not a fixed destiny or fate, the causes that have not yet matured can be weakened, changed, and even made useful. It calls for great human maturity, however, and here, humane religions of experience may be at a disadvantage. Because they do not force their ideologies on others, Buddhist societies often coexist with dogmatic ideologies. Medieval Tibet was a perfect example of mistaken permissiveness. There Buddha's teachings were protected and flourished among free yogis while the monasteries fought and the rest of society employed barbaric punishments. Though often called for, non-dogmatic religions have little power or motivation to influence the societies in which they work.

Whoever wants to avoid thoughtless reactions to unpleasant events should above all learn to create space, to stretch out the moment before anything is done or said. During that time a conscious decision can be made to ensure that a meaningful action helps others mature and avoids further trouble. As Buddha's 84,000 teachings relate only to mind and how to realize it, they apply everywhere and in all situations. In time and with enough experience, one can recognize arising causes of pain and deflect them.

Buddha's third Noble Truth, "There is an end to suffering," is especially inspiring in the West today. This awareness, above all, fits the altruistic disposition expressed in our societies. Standing fast in the timeless experience of his power, Buddha confirmed to the five seekers in Sarnath that enlightenment exists and that he had achieved it. Having reached the ultimate goal, the perfect state he was continuously experiencing, for the first time in history there was something real and absolute to strive for, a timeless and true refuge for all.

Buddha has not dwelt alone in such fulfilment. Since that time, many who developed through his methods and views have come to know their minds. Because of his transmission, which continues today, inspired teachers continue to experience and confirm parts or all of his highest insight.

Buddha's teachings unceasingly point to mind's ultimate nature. They show its essence to be all knowing fearless space and turn one's steady experience into continual highest joy. From such surplus, every act is powerful, looks far into the future, and expresses non-discriminating but prospective and unsentimental compassion. It is the motivation of a statesman rather than that of a politician, a motivation that is focused on retaining timeless achievements and other essential human values.

In the Deer Park at Sarnath, a large stupa, dilapidated due to a Turkish Muslim invasion during the twelfth century, still celebrates the event of Buddha finally sharing his fourth Noble Truth, "There are ways to the ending of suffering, a path to enlightenment." Such ways offered to ordinary people, as well as to the many highly intelligent students that came to him over the next forty five years, have given a billion people Buddhism, produced many convincing teachers, and brought countless beings meaningful lives.

Buddha's timelessly valid methods to end suffering and bring about the full functioning of body, speech, and mind enable one to lead others to fulfilment. In spite of the many miracles Buddha performed to dissolve his students' fixed ideas, he always called his teachings his true legacy, because they enable all who wish to become like him. Based on an understanding of cause and effect, they unfold during the expansion of a rich inner life and are realized through holding the pure view. Seeing things as they really are and developing step-by-step, every experience becomes a mirror to one's mind. This is what this book is about.

Karma — Cause and Effect

Whoever wants to think that society, a god with no sense of humor, other people, a devil, or simply accidents cause bad things to happen, will find many spiritual offers. Buddha's teachings, however, will not be among them. Every decent school of Buddhism teaches self responsibility: Whatever one sows one will also harvest, if one does not remove or transform the karmic seeds beforehand. Here one learns to understand one's present situation and experiences the results of former thoughts, words, and actions without looking for guilty parties elsewhere. One thereby becomes the conscious master of one's life and can begin to effectively sow seeds for future happiness. Thus people are freed from being children forever, dependent upon and passively delivered over to murky causes and unclear circumstances.

Whoever wants to create a lasting and unshakeable foundation for one's life only needs to focus on the law of cause and effect. The impressions that are planted in everyone's subconscious or energy fields, through one's actions of body, speech, and mind, will mature in their own time. Outer and inner conditions will come together, deciding one's future, and influencing the outer world. Even though many events, like the weather and the economy, are determined by numerous conditions and are therefore difficult to fully fathom, they still express ripening layers of cause and effect.

Such insights change one's understanding of the world's joys and troubles. With the Middle Eastern concept of having only one life, which has been dominant in Europe over the last 1,000 years, much of what happens must be deemed accidental or unjust. If it is not understood that mind is a beginningless stream of impressions held together by the illusion of a self and that the law of causality is active before, during, and after this existence, one has no way to find meaning in events. It is therefore very useful to share Buddha's insights into causality, called the *law of karma*, in which all unenlightened beings are trapped.

At death, when perceptions disappear along with the sense organs, the impressions stored in one's subconsciousness during one's last existence surface, bringing about four results. They first decide one's experience between one human body and the next. If desire was the dead person's strongest tendency, mind's attraction to a mother's womb at the moment of conception will take place within seven weeks. If other feelings were prominent, the conditions for a new human birth may only appear after long stays in other mental realms. Secondly, these impressions attract mind to its future parents, with genetics that fit. Thirdly, they determine the outer conditions of one's rebirth, whether in Switzerland or the

Congo. And fourthly, they continue as the attitude with which one encounters the world and other beings. This disposition once again leads to useful and harmful actions, which then mature into subsequent lives.

In this context it may disturb well meaning people that, despite all the supportive efforts by the West today, the main collective suffering of the world still happens in Africa and other countries around the equator. But people do not need to be afraid of finding racist views in Buddhism. Karma is changeable. The teachings state clearly that all sentient beings have buddha nature, that their minds are essentially clear light, whether cultures or situations help or block their chance of experiencing it. While Buddha lived in a highly developed culture, Northern Europeans, whose culture is imitated worldwide today, still once fought each other with stone axes. Certain conditions do however create environments where beings find it more difficult to exist, learn positive values, or practice humanistic teachings. Karma is also sticky: Even if people move from an area that is oppressive to a kinder society, many still do not benefit because they simply bring their suppressed habits and behaviors with them. This is very noticeable around the world today. The only way to leave karma at the roadside is to consciously choose better values and actually behave differently.

Buddha praised ten useful actions and advised against their ten harmful opposites. They concern our totality: body, speech and mind. Here is a quick and modern interpretation of them. Use the body to protect, be generous, and for the layperson, to give sexual happiness. Avoid using it to kill, rob, break apart functioning relationships, or sexually harm others. Employ speech positively to show people how to live in the world, cooperate, communicate well, and to share meaningful insights. Avoid lies that harm others or misrepresent one's spiritual accomplishments, splitting people by slandering, rough talk, and gossip. Positively, concerning mind, Buddha's advice is to wish everybody happiness, share in good acts done by others, and think clearly. One should at all costs avoid turning one's mind to hate, envy, and wrong views. These are not commandments. Everyone is free to decide whether they want to guide their lives by such advice or not.

The five seekers in Sarnath were the kind of people who hoped to avoid their own suffering. For this they needed to understand the teachings of the Four Noble Truths and Buddha's instructions on cause and effect. As far as they could trust it, their new knowledge, especially of pain inducing actions and the calming and holding meditations that Buddha taught, reduced their troubles and gave them a protective inner distance to events. With such information they could move towards liberation by understanding that there exists no lasting or vulnerable *me* or *self* in neither body, feelings, nor thoughts. The secure state, where such realization keeps one from feeling like the target, is called liberation. This path and its corresponding point of view is called the Small Way (Sanskrit: *Hinayana*, Tibetan: *Thegchung*). It became predominant in the southern Buddhist countries of Asia.

People from European oriented welfare societies often see the Small Way as being for monks and nuns, that it doesn't allow them to express their full potential in life. They are more attracted to the second group of teachings of the Buddha, called the Great Way (Sanskrit: *Mahayana,* Tibetan: *Thegchen*). The goal of its methods is full enlightenment for the benefit of all beings and liberation happens as a gift while working for others. This motivation puts the happiness of others ahead of one's own and those on the Great Way come to enjoy rich inner lives. They easily develop a healthy mix of compassion and wisdom.

At Buddha's time, like today, there were many whose potential was not exhausted by striving only for inner peace. They too were sharply aware of impermanence and noticed the dreamlike, empty, and conditioned nature of all phenomena, inner as well as outer. While probing the unreality of the outer world, they realized that beings are innumerable and want happiness, whereas they themselves were merely each a single being. Such insight automatically develops into brave and altruistic acts by beings and their societies.

A third level of Buddha's students are the main focus of this book and the driving force of Buddhism in the West today. Their special quality is the power to see the teacher as an expression of perfection and a mirror to their own minds. Confident in the teacher's example as means to recognize one's inherent buddha nature, they also understand that one can only perceive perfection outside because one has this potential in oneself. As such students are prepared to behave like buddhas until they become buddhas. From ancient times until today, skillful lamas are able to teach them in complete ways. Involving all aspects of body, speech, and mind as a totality, these methods constitute the absolute level. Here one identifies, to the best of one's ability, with the highest level of awareness; seeing oneself and all beings as buddhas and bodhisattvas and the outer world as a perfect pure land. Experiencing thoughts as wisdom and sounds as mantras, this is the exciting and transformative Buddhism that inspires even the wildest Westerners.

Called *Mantrayana* for its work with vibrations, and *Tantrayana* for totally encompassing all of life's situations, the main term used for these absolute teachings is Diamond Way. Though diamonds are said to be a girl's best friend, the term was not chosen to bring ladies to lay Kagyu centers. It is the literal translation of *Vajrayana* in Sanskrit and *Dorje Thegpa* in Tibetan. Its methods are exceedingly quick if one is willing to establish its pure view. Though the goal is the same as that of the Great Way, full enlightenment, the Diamond Way method of identifying with perfection as one's true essence is ultimate. It is thus different from both the Small and the Great Ways, where the relative aspect of working towards the goal is predominant. The best approach is all three ways together, as advised also by the Dalai Lama, to outwardly do as little harm as possible, inwardly to balance compassion and wisdom, and secretly keep the highest view.

The one goal of all Buddhist teachings is thus for everyone to develop, making the vast differences among these three views and methods into different steps on the same path. As life is short and one has today the chance to be informed on all levels, one should enter on the highest level that one can effectively use and develop, while also solidifying one's foundation. The difference between a buddha and an unenlightened being is only that the former knows both mind and what it brings forth, while the latter just sees what comes and goes, inwardly as well as externally. Having freed himself from all faults and painful habits, and having opened up to all beings, Buddha became perfect.

The Great Way —
Uniting Compassion and Wisdom

Eight years after his first teaching on the Four Noble Truths in Sarnath, completely different types of people came to Buddha's dwelling near Rajgir at Vulture's Peak, which lies a few hours by bus from Bodhgaya. These hundreds of students were potential bodhisattvas, people with an emotional surplus for others and capable of a broad, beyond personal attitude. Because of their maturity and life experience, Buddha had rich material with which to work. In tandem with their inherent compassion, Buddha could unlock their rich and innate wisdom. As a result, without getting trapped in either hopes or fears, these students learned to see both how things are and how they appear to be.

Compassion

As explained in the Small Way, whoever pays attention to cause and effect and understands the non-reality of a self can achieve a liberated state where one is no longer the target. For the infinitely larger goal of enlightenment in the Great Way, where the mutable conditions of the outer world must also be realized, all encompassing and non-discriminating compassion is an unconditional prerequisite. Here one needs to be motivated by the desire for all beings to experience happiness.

In the Great Way, one's interaction with the world constantly refreshes and strengthens this motivation. Love of this kind is always the ultimate. Generous in expression and leaving no space for expectation or tightness in any situation, it grows into the highest of realization. Every meditation of the Great Way begins with this fresh motivation and ends with the wish that all accumulated good impressions may become limitless and reach everyone. Also on the practical level, each experienced happiness is passed on several times during the day to everybody.

Eskimos in Greenland have twenty words for different kinds of snow. Our culture, technical as it is, has hundreds of designations for parts of machines that help us master the world. If we look inward, however, a similar view is clearly lacking. We use changing and unclear terms for inner states of mind and have no understanding of its totality. Buddha, in his time, was completely methodical and encompassing in his description of mind.

In the Great Way, Buddha described four kinds of love, called the Four Immeasurables, and emphasized three kinds of compassion beyond worldly joy and equanimity. As these qualities become spontaneous, they offer one essential pillar for using the most effective methods. The second and balancing column, exact and non-sentimental, is the beyond personal wisdom. Together they offer the conditions for the third and absolute level, the total transformation and knowing of mind in the Diamond Way.

The first of the four kinds of love is the wish that everyone may be happy. In normal life this includes the romantic love that is so essential to beings. Here people find each other attractive and use their bodies, speech, and mind to give their partners every possible joy. Through this love one develops new qualities and inspires one's surroundings. The fulfillment of love gives people a first taste of the ultimate joy of enlightenment. The traditional wish expressing it is, "May all beings have happiness and its cause."

The second kind of love is compassion. Here one shares a surplus of something meaningful without any personal expectations. Compassion enables one to remove the pain of beings and through this example, many find their own power of generosity. Compassion must never be confused with theistic pity, which is wholly unconstructive, puts beings down, and leaves little room for improvement.

Three precious expressions of compassion motivate three practical expressions of kindness: that of the king, the ferryman, and the herdsman. Any one may be chosen, but it is advisable to start with what is closest to one's nature. First and well known throughout history, but tragic if the ego has not transcended, is the role of the king. In the best case a king thinks, "When I am strong, I will benefit everyone." Then, there is the compassion of the ferryman. He takes everyone along thinking, "Now we all leave confusion and together go to the shore of human growth." Finally, in religions that flatter their adherents by comparing them to sheep, there is the role of a herdsman. He habitually thinks of others before himself. He lives by the idea: Whoever thinks of himself has difficulties, but whoever thinks of others has interesting tasks to do. Because the real trick for freeing mind is to forget the illusory self, the herdsman may reach the goal first. Whichever approach is right for each individual should be used. It has surely developed over many lives and is the best way for them.

Although compassion arises naturally from a certain level of development, it is still useful to activate it consciously. It is easiest to develop good feelings for those who already fulfill one's expectations. Many surely experience this type of compassion. It is a bigger challenge to wish others happiness when they repeat mistakes, are obnoxious, or behave like enemies. The key to developing compassion for these people is to understand that the root cause of their behavior is ignorance, not evil. Suffering arises from acting or speaking short sightedly. More people grab the stinging nettles than the flowers of life. Ultimately everyone wants happiness but few know how to bring it about. Buddha taught in order to change that. The traditional phrase expressing compassion is, "May all beings be without suffering and its cause."

The third Immeasurable is called sympathetic joy. It is the wish for others not only to be happy and avoid suffering in an ordinary sense, but also to progress from passing and conditional joys to the ultimate happiness of enlightenment. The classic formulation of beyond worldly joy is, "May they always experience highest joy, which is totally beyond suffering."

This third kind of loving feeling is experienced when one simply feels happy about something good taking place for others. A most meaningful example of this would be the deep joy when impoverished and over populated countries reduce their birth rates. Since this results in fewer mouths to feed, more freedom for women, and a better quality of life for all, there is no finer way to help. An impressive surge of this feeling occurred in Europe in 1989 when the Berlin Wall fell; so many shared the ecstasy when the freshly liberated masses could finally spill into West Berlin.

The fourth kind of love is its culmination called equanimity. This means the limitless understanding that everyone possesses buddha nature, regardless of whatever incomprehensible and pain producing deeds some may perform. Being essentially space, mind's essence can neither be destroyed nor changed. Even behind the sick images in the minds of a Mao, a Stalin, a Hitler, a Khomeini, or a Pol Pot is some space and awareness that may, after massive purifications, meet with enlightened teachings and recognize itself. This last of these four dispositions is traditionally expressed, "May they be without attachment to some and aversion against others, but feel the same love for all."

Transcending anything personal, these four expressions of love radiate on all beings like the sun. Undisturbed, they make one simply do the right thing and accomplish what is in front of one's nose. Spontaneously bringing about everything good that others' karma and talents make possible, they are an immense gift to all. Such non-differentiating compassion is limitless and perfect. It expresses the interdependence of all phenomena and Buddha's love for all beings.

Love must be combined with intuitive insight for full accomplishment to be reached. Wonderful feelings are not enough. The nature of things must also be understood. Love without wisdom leads to dogma and sentimentality while the one-sided development of wisdom makes for a cold, calculating, and humorless individual. As both hands and eyes are needed to accomplish most things in the world, compassion and wisdom must be balanced in the Great Way.

Wisdom

There are two types of wisdom. The first, worldly wisdom, focuses on whatever happens in mind. It concerns outer and inner phenomena and is like images in mind's mirror. The other enlightening wisdom refers directly to mind and its radiant awareness.

Worldly wisdom is taught in schools and universities. It enables people to earn more money in a shorter time, to do exciting jobs, to meet more interesting people, and to die with more debt than those who are less educated. This wisdom is limited to what is impermanent and its advantages are lost at death. Even during life, the knowledge gained on the worldly level of concepts does not bring true happiness, and hard won riches are worthwhile only for small amounts of time or as means for doing something really meaningful. "The last shirt has no pockets," as a Danish proverb goes. However, training one's mind is of the utmost use also for future lives. At the time of conception, one's consciousness will then be naturally drawn to gifted parents and, with their genetic heritage and a good upbringing, one stands a good chance for a full and rich life, maybe even for the benefit of many.

The liberating and enlightening wisdom of knowing mind brings lasting meaning and joy. Though obscured since beginningless time, it can never be lost! The essence of mind is space: open, clear and limitless. Because mind has never been born and also cannot die, its qualities are unconditional and timeless. From one life to the next, any parts of mind's mirror that have once been cleaned, easily become clear again. Thus beyond personal capacities can grow, inspiring all around.

But how may mind know itself? By feeding it even more ideas and concepts? No, on the contrary, the way to enlightenment lies beyond thoughts. Even learned Buddhist monks from Tibet, who may debate philosophical texts for days on end, can add nothing to truth nature. Mind's timeless essence, its awareness, emerges by being that which is between and behind the thoughts and knows them. When the experiencer rests fully conscious in the space of awareness, recognizing everything outer and inner as its free play, that is the ultimate result.

First the liberating realization of non-ego arises from the state of radiant awareness and being undisturbed by any event. When the enlightening wisdom of the non-reality of anything outer follows, mind cuts through all duality. Knowing subject, object, and action to be aspects of the same totality and also interdependent, no part of mind can again become neurotic and all perfect qualities and activities must arise. The world is experienced as it is, empty of any lasting nature. At the same time it appears as an infinite and constantly changing flow of causes and effects.

From their growing awareness that such states may be reached, wise people dedicate themselves to whatever practice produces spiritual growth. Those who do not discover mind's full potential deprive themselves of meaning and the bliss of increasing perfection. The reason for this is tragic ignorance, which can be described as consisting of four or two obscuring veils, obstacles to recognizing minds true state. These correspond to Buddha's second Noble Truth, "Suffering has a cause."

Following the notion of four veils obscuring mind, one distinguishes as follows:

- Because unenlightened mind works like an eye, seeing everything outside but not itself, one makes the basic mistake of holding a dualistic viewpoint.
- The main disturbing emotions that unfold from that viewpoint are ignorance, attachment, and aversion. They cause pride, greed, and envy, which again give rise to a total of 84,000 mixed mental states.
- By taking such changing and conditioned causes to be real, confused words and deeds, as well as all unwholesome activities, follow from these disturbing emotions.
- These actions bring about short sighted habits and painful

results. Like a wheel turning, these results again motivate beings to further unskillful actions or words, which, if not neutralized or transformed, produce future painful situations.

Seen from the viewpoint of two veils, the first one is attachment to mind's constantly changing states and disturbing emotions. Whoever wavers between conditioned happiness and suffering, between liking and disliking, will get no inkling of their innate Truth State. They will experience little of the depth of meaning that pervades everything. The second veil is one's stiff ideas, the mistaken but pervading concept that the perceiving mind, subject, and perceived object are separate. This cramps one's direct awareness. In this state words and ideas can only be shadows of experience, not experience itself. Clinging to concepts makes one miss the experience. A finger pointing to the moon is not the moon.

Whichever of the above models one uses to understand the obstacles on one's way, mind will recognize its essence when all obscuring influences are removed. As long as mind is unable to perceive itself as all pervading and the container of all things, a feeling of separation from totality will remain. Whoever is willing to give up the illusion of a separate and existing *me*, frees oneself. The insight that there is no real or lasting essence or self inside or outside one's body that one must care about, no true target for suffering provides increasing distance from one's disturbing emotions. The potential of space itself then becomes an exciting friend.

With enough good impressions activated, it becomes possible to also remove mind's final veil, one's dualistic clinging to the separation of subject and object. Once being and non-being are seen as two aspects of the same totality, the highest realization of enlightenment is reached. Here mind's blissful and kind potential will freely unfold.

Disturbing Emotions — Sources of Wisdom

Buddha used difficult mental states, seen as immoral or unsocial by varying religions and worldviews, as raw material and conscious tools for the inner and secret development of his students. By means of a series of teachings and skillful methods, which have become a rich source of wisdom to contemporary psychology and philosophy, disturbing feelings are transformed into the wisdoms that reside within them. In Diamond Way teachings, one uses the force of strong emotions as fuel for development.

Buddha's teachings mention 84,000 conditioned states of consciousness and mental veils, all leading to clumsy and harmful actions and words. These arise through various combinations of the five main disturbing emotions; ignorance, pride, desire, jealousy, and anger. In the painting of the Wheel of Life, held by the jaws of impermanence, desire and greed are separate and therefore six disturbing feelings are counted. They cause the six realms of existence, through which beings alternate until mind recognizes itself.

Buddha advises a three step recycling of these imaginary but tenacious enemies. In the Small Way, a state of mindfulness is developed. One becomes conscious of mixed emotions as soon as they arise. This early warning system effectively helps one weaken or avoid the conditions bringing such feelings about and painful dramas are avoided. It gives a person the space to improve gradually and privately, instead of publicly losing face.

Continuing on the Great Way, the second step is to understand the transitory, conditioned, and composite nature of disturbing emotions. Five minutes ago they were not here, and experience tells us that five minutes later they will again disappear or lose their power. It is therefore foolish to get involved with mental states that are both embarrassing and constantly changing. Using the Great Way, whoever notices disturbing feelings in time can investigate them at arm's length. Recognizing the pattern behind them steadily deprives such states of their persuasive power. The freedom that everyone can attain is then consciously grasped, and life can be shaped according to one's own wishes.

If self pity is a player, it helps to compare one's own life situation with that of others. Such feelings become embarrassing when one considers what life is like in most of Africa or how children are used as suicide bombers in terrorist activities. Thoughts like, "Would I like to trade places with him?" or, "I have to suffer her for only five minutes, but she has to live with herself the whole time," or, "Why is he trying to become my patient?" give one space during unpleasant but non-threatening encounters. The security felt by giving oneself space allows one to give ever wiser and more compassionate feedback to people who are obviously suffering.

Buddhists are generally aware that beings act foolishly because of ignorance rather than out of genuine malice. It is certainly old shared karmas that make people meet in dramatic ways as aggressors and victims, the former acquiring and the latter losing bad karma. Therefore one should act precisely and protectively, but have compassion for all. For such reasons, stupidity and confusion count as disturbing emotions in Buddhism. They are the causes of all other painful states. This understanding is not evident to most religions. Yet if one observes the results of such mental veils, this cause and effect relationship becomes obvious. For example, everybody has unwittingly caused suffering to others because they could not foresee the consequences of their own actions or words and many well-intentioned people fail in their idealistic efforts because they lack an overview. Once one consciously relaxes into space, intuitive inspiration and clarity will show that everything is mind and therefore inseparable. Confusion appears from the mistaken experiencing of subject, object, and action as separate and independent of each other.

Even if one may not understand quantum physics, all sixteen levels of the emptiness of phenomena, or the interdependent origination of all appearances as taught by Buddha, by consciously abiding at one's center of experience and simply being aware, ignorance will naturally transform into human maturity. Those who are unable to study at length may successfully use this approach to cultivate a rich inner life.

Mind functions in totally holistic and subtle ways. Buddahood is not reached through the number of books one reads, but through one's view and experiences during life. A person will be fine if one studies the general outline of the teachings, meditates according to the given instructions, and adheres to healthy reasoning rather than hiding fearfully and irresponsibly behind the games of political correctness. The less energy and time are needed to handle self imposed difficulties, the better. Then one is not distracted for too long from meaningful subjects and moving on is more easily accomplished. Unless one is under emotional stress, following the idea, "First thought, best thought!" usually produces the smoothest results. If one stays in the stream of life and observes cause and effect, the practical qualities unfolding from direct experience will replace missing concepts.

The tendency to enrich the imagined *me* to obtain lasting joy leads many people to experience attachment and greed. Generosity is the liberating antidote to these disturbing emotions. In this practice one habitually wishes the best for others regardless of one's own conditions, understanding that beings are countless, and therefore more important than oneself. Through this most important activity which influences desire, attachment, expectations, greed, and avarice, good karmic connections will appear. Impermanence is also useful to raise one's awareness of all conditioned joys. It enables people to share some physical joys with others and do things for the benefit of all. Only enlightenment is timeless highest joy, and it hardly matters whether one is driven to the grave in a Mazda or a Mercedes.

The protective function of the illusory *I*, expressing itself as aversion, ill will, anger, and hatred, is transformed through love and compassion. When anger arises, one should quickly become aware of it and when in danger of a sudden outburst, conquer it during the surge. If that is impossible, one may also try to sidetrack the feeling and thereby avoid embarrassing dramas. It is wiser not to speak or act in a moment of anger. Be the big dog instead. They don't need to bark.

Opponents and difficult people are usually more confused or misinformed than malicious. On top of this, they have to live with themselves day and night. Adding to such misfortune would not be sportsmanlike. Instead, by understanding that non-meditators react more from their own mental states than to the actual world, one may meet any unpleasant situation with a wide and compassionate view. Drawing down any angry feelings and learning from the process, one will become a useful example. Most important of all, however, is to forgive and let go. Otherwise a bond remains and they will appear again.

The idea of being better than others leads to exclusive pride. But since there is surely someone in the world that is quicker, stronger, smarter, or a more attentive lover, one might as well relax. It is much more satisfying to focus on everyone's buddha nature and the unlimited potential of all beings. This view is the perfect antidote against a feeling that otherwise makes gifted people stiff and bitter. An important insight is that heaven and hell happen between one's ears or ribs, or wherever people suspect their minds to be, and not elsewhere. The joy felt by experiencing others as exciting and interesting increases and is lasting, whereas always focusing on others' mistakes brings spiritual poverty. Then one is always in bad company and neither others nor oneself is inspired to develop any of one's inborn capacities. It is a question of view and habit, whether the glass is seen as half full or half empty.

The belief that one is entitled to more leads to jealousy or envy. Jealousy is a particularly stubborn customer. It takes nourishment from anything but also survives without any support at all. Green and ugly, it often sneaks subliminally through mind for a long time. At the same time, however, to a conscious person it offers an object for prolonged observation and may bring one to understand how other feelings arise and function. For these reasons, jealousy is a first class guinea pig for testing one's spiritual development. Its power to influence clearly shows how an independent consciousness has grown out of its passing impressions. The following cure, which brings deep and quick relief, is to wish the object of one's envy so much of what one envies, that it reaches the level of a fairytale. For example to wish them limousines so long that they can hardly park them, the most exciting jobs imaginable, a hundred choir girls or athletic officers visiting every night, and the health and time needed to enjoy it all.

How does knowledge about disturbing emotions aid practically in everyday life? Though most beings have all the disturbing emotions, Buddha distinguishes between three main types or dispositions: desire types, anger/pride types, and confusion types.

Desire Types. Whoever has many wishes, attachments, and desires is predisposed for joy simply because one's mind is oriented toward pleasant things and happiness. While naturally protecting this disposition from early on in life, it is essential to learn to live with the understanding that everything conditioned is impermanent and only mind will last. This viewpoint produces a thick skin and a basic generosity, which provides the space and momentum for directly passing on every good feeling. Each moment overflows with meaning when shared from a big heart, and others are invited to partake in whatever good is experienced. Desire is the general karmic cause for a human rebirth.

Anger Types. Those who are deeply or frequently disappointed or who habitually block their own power, often experience envy and anger. They then develop the tendency to notice everything they don't like and spread bad feelings even without wanting to do so. Here Buddha's advice is to develop compassion for others and to understand that maybe those who make mistakes cannot help it. If that doesn't work, one can also think that these same people may die tomorrow so there is only this one chance to be good to them.

It is important to remember, also historically, how ignorant people are of cause and effect, and that study is no alternative to genuine life experience. Everyone wants happiness and wants to feel good, but immature views and self-made obstacles make people gather life's thistles instead of its flowers. Compassion must arise when seeing the mess people so often make out of their unlimited potential. Then without pity or sentimentality, one does what one can for others.

Confusion Types. The best advice for those who are mainly hindered by confusion is the so-called salami technique. While handling life slice-by-slice, and day-by-day, one should deliberate as little as possible and try to accomplish what is directly in front of one's nose. Continuing like this, experience will gradually arise and the workings of causality become evident. Practically, this means to do one's best every moment while learning from the results as best as one can, but not to freeze like an old horse or crocodile that doesn't know if it's coming or going.

The above three mindsets become evident at Christmas, when many tendencies surface. Desire types leave imprints of their noses on the shop windows to catch up on everything. Anger people cause commotion walking in the middle of the street in order to arrogantly avoid the childish window gazers and the confused types zigzag in and out, not sure what they like or dislike. While one also meets those who are predominately proud, envious or stingy, the three types already described are central. Pride springs from ignorance, envy from anger, and stinginess from attachment.

The unique power of turning disturbing feelings into wisdom resides on the third, ultimate, and consequential level of Buddhism, its Diamond Way. Here every tool of body, speech, and mind is used. As the ordinary world is transformed into a pure land, every disturbing mental state is uprooted to the level of ultimate purity. The teachings recognize highest joy as highest truth and the perfect level of functioning. Therefore one may treat disturbances as a silly film that one simply chooses not to watch, or view mixed feelings as a zoo leaving one's mind. It provides deep relief that one is seeing the backs and not the faces of the strange animals that are neuroses on their way out. Staying stubbornly with what is here and now, annoyances will wither for lack of acknowledgment.

As one's practice increasingly succeeds over the years, one recognizes with the fresh joy of discovery that painful feelings do not simply disappear in mind's ocean, but rather transform into something radiant and meaningful. They change into Five Liberating Wisdoms. In the same way garbage may become excellent fertilizer, one's worst mental disturbances now produce a rich abundance of insight.

How does this transformation happen? When unexpressed anger dissolves in mind, all is seen as clearly as in a mirror. Nothing is added nor is anything taken away. Exclusive pride is transformed into the experience of the many sidedness and basic richness of all things. Attachment becomes discriminating wisdom, the ability to understand processes or beings both in their uniqueness and as parts of a whole. Jealousy, secretly busying itself with anticipation or sticking to the past, turns out to be the wisdom of experience. Finally, the way clouds disappear into rain, confusion itself dissolves into all pervading wisdom. Because one is not separated from anything, one then knows that information, space, and energy are all united, everywhere and always.

Whoever perceives the dissolution of disturbing emotions as mind's self liberation and has the power to observe their passing without being sucked into useless and time consuming actions or words, will realize an ocean of accomplishment. Clumsy inner states, for so long seemingly invincible enemies, will appear as wellsprings of power. Working with the coal dust of ordinary situations, one will produce the most beautiful of diamonds.

The Diamond Way — All Tools in Use

As mentioned earlier, Buddha taught the Four Noble Truths at Sarnath and gave the inner teachings of compassion and wisdom near Rajgir in Northern India. Many of his ultimate Diamond Way teachings that work on the secret and deepest levels were given near Vaishali, also in North Eastern India. Involving body, speech, and mind, and building on the inherent buddha nature of all, they are known foremost for their holistic and extremely effective methods.

Buddha used every moment to teach. Whenever exciting people, rich in life experience and joy sought him out, there were amazing meetings where he transmitted to them a timeless experience of their mind. The inherent closeness of these students to enlightenment and their ability to experience Buddha as in no way external or separate from themselves unceasingly blessed and motivated them. Their strong devotion enabled them to see Buddha as a mirror to their own mind and in this way they quickly absorbed his qualities. They experienced the radiantly aware space between thoughts, the Great Seal (Sanskrit: *Mahamudra*), as their own true essence. This freed up a surplus of joy and power that had grown in them over many lifetimes.

Devotion has many sides. Although the free peoples of the world choose the politicians that they hope will best express their tendencies and expectations, karma ultimately decides which leaders these people actually get. In the case of religions, however, devotion is an extra and frequently very wild card. Life gives people little overview of the matter, immensely increasing the responsibility of teachers. Touching profound human expectations and frequently irrational, religions are more difficult to evaluate than political or social systems. If one encounters a religion or teacher that corresponds to one's own deepest nature, one is unavoidably drawn to it. After all, one sees one's own face! It is therefore important to understand and when necessary counteract the immense power of religious devotion and its root cause, the experience of recognition.

The core feeling in a religion is definitive, be it beautiful or ugly, liberating or oppressive, and triggers people's feelings from which their actions later spring. Because even angry people basically want some kind of happiness and because negative emotions destroy the effectiveness of all who have them, free societies improve. In the long run, the holders of compassionate teachings must become willing and able to defend themselves. Their environment makes people develop consciously and for the benefit of all. Whoever treasures that space, expressed through their teacher's fearlessness, and freely uses its abundance of experience and methods, enjoys a direct access to enlightenment.

The Four Realms of Buddha Activities

All buddhas, continually and effortlessly, employ their body, speech, mind, qualities, and activities to help others. This produces the greatest advantage for the highest number of beings, into the most distant future. When no separation is felt between the doer, the action, and the object, each moment's potential is playfully realized. Each situation is a constantly fresh experiencing of "Aha!" and "How rich is life!"

Buddha's effective insights, meditations, and means against various mental veils and disturbing emotions still exist and bring beings four ways of consciously turning events in a positive direction. Known as peace giving, enriching, fascinating, and powerfully protecting, they place the finest of tools in one's hands to transform every aspect of life and turn every experience into a step to enlightenment. As space is information and everyone affects the world, consciously turning one's activities in a useful direction creates happiness and meaning for all.

The peace giving activity is like a jovial host that will not rest until everyone is satisfied. Teachers with these activities are usually very sensitive. Often with the tendency to acquire a body shape of a pear, they have to watch out not to be used by others or harm themselves by too much time spent at the table. If they stay clear of that, they can bring a lot of people the love and warmth they may have lacked. As early as possible, however, one should direct the emotional openness developed through this to a lasting, beyond personal, and meaningful level.

The physical appearance of the enriching type is often quite different. He has thin bones, moves fast, and is constantly aware of what is going on in all the practical levels he creates. Since he has the ability to reach and connect with many people, he should not only focus on the latest new trend, but instead develop a liberating view that will make him a true friend. This is much more meaningful and fulfilling than constantly chasing materialistic values.

The fascinating activity is especially easy for attractive people. Quickly recognized by others, using one's beauty makes sense. It is the result of compassionate acts during past lives and therefore appeals to many. By simply using this gift on a superficial level, everyone loses the most precious thing there is: time.

The powerfully protecting type is the true friend of all beings. He is unshakeable and his body and speech express these qualities. His eyes are perceptive and he is prepared for any development in space. When the other three types are already busy elsewhere, he will stay behind to finish things. Although not too concerned about his looks and bored by the daily gossip, he is the pillar that people can rely upon.

How can a teacher incorporate this knowledge? By skillfully developing the potential for these four activities in themselves and others. It is no secret that most prefer the activities that fit in with their own natural qualities, and that they attract similar types of students. Learned or cultural groups tend to appear around the teachers of the Great Way, while the wilder types, who desire direct experience, seek out the Diamond Way.

Peace-giving. If students are fragile or simply difficult, it is advisable to give them space, especially those who have something to prove. If they can be kept on a sidetrack without passing on their attitude to others, many will explode from a lack of attention. A teacher can then help them rearrange better patterns of behavior and help create a more pleasant future.

Enriching. Having produced a secure situation for people with a basis for further growth, the teacher's function evolves into increasing the richness and potential of the students' lives. Usually this should happen step-by-step. Especially when inexperienced people try to go too fast or to accomplish too much and then fall on their hopeful noses, the illusory ego quickly strengthens its position. In the Diamond Way, where the development of all of mind's qualities is the goal, the above two areas of activity are easy to oversee. The teacher only needs to observe whether the students are becoming independent, developing a robust and joyful attitude towards sex and life, and if they are exhibiting an excess of energy for others.

Fascinating. If one has the power to influence others, great spiritual growth becomes possible. However, this ability can also create much harm. If one's training starts too early, is overly political, or teaches ideas that are contrary to basic human wishes, it must be considered indoctrination. This type of influence will harden a mind for a lifetime. Religious scandals around the world are nothing new and probably no literate person expects anything but hate and suppression from totalitarian religions. But scandals have also been caused by some worthy monks and teachers in Buddha's good name. Although Buddha's instructions are advice from an enlightened friend and not commandments from a dogmatic god, it still seems difficult for some to carry Buddha's example into the world. A teacher should avoid every act that disturbs the trusting relationship with a student and should avoid wasting time on meaningless luxury. Above all one should never been seen to take more pride in oneself than in one's lineage and transmission. Most importantly embarrassments discourage the growing number of idealistic minds that now turn to Buddhism.

Powerfully protecting. Powerfully protective actions are the fourth type of buddha activity and they too demand constant self-examination. The negative feelings of anger, ill will, and hatred when engaged in controlling, and if necessary, destroying activity require one's full attention. Only those who see the potential buddha in others can rough them up without making mistakes.

Teachers who give their body, speech, and mind to protect others must make sure that their actions or words are not colored by their personal dislikes. One should be like a good doctor who does not operate to enhance his own fame, but only to avoid a later and greater harm to his patient. It takes true responsibility for a teacher to use this effective tool, since most expect true spirituality to be uncritical, sweet, and peaceful. Therefore, it remains a cowardly and a serious breach of responsibility for a teacher to ignore his ability to see further and to give real guidance. Whoever hopes to avoid a small immediate conflict by refusing to face threatening developments in the world will leave others defenseless. A teacher working within the two last activities of fascination and powerfully protecting activity must therefore be especially responsible. Above all this person must be informed of the facts and also constantly check that his own attitude is to benefit others. Only those teachers who dare to be unsentimental and to put their popularity on the line are trustworthy. They are truly free and their work will benefit and develop others in the long run.

Methods in the Diamond Way

Who received Buddha's third and ultimate level of teachings? The students who saw Buddha as neither a god nor a human, but as a mirror to their own minds possessed the necessary openness to enter and benefit from the Diamond Way transmission. Because their devotion made them experience Buddha as totally close and familiar, they automatically absorbed both his formed way of meditating on the buddha aspects and his highest view of the Great

Seal, thus gradually awakening their own inherent enlightened qualities. Towards that ultimate goal, Buddha applied numerous effective methods, which are still known and used to this day. They provide an unbroken stream of living insight from teacher to student.

All Diamond Way methods presuppose a prepared mind and the wish to practice for the benefit of all beings. At the outset of any meditation, one takes refuge, consciously and deeply. It begins, protects, and guides all Buddhist practices. One also develops the enlightened attitude, the wish for the full realization of all beings. Through the building up phase, where a lama or buddha is called to the meditator's mind, one releases troublesome impressions and accumulates countless useful ones. This strengthens one's openness to the principle of the teacher. The schools of Tibetan Buddhism here advocate the *Ngondro*, a set of foundational meditation practices. The three old, or Red Hat, schools aim for a quick and intuitive understanding of the teachings while the reformed monastic Yellow Hat School first pursues a lengthy intellectual comprehension. The main parts of these meditations are repeated 111,111 times and are tantric, which means that they employ all aspects of body, speech, and mind at one time.

In the Diamond Way, after having completed the Ngondro, mind has three strong levels for recognizing itself. The direct *Way of Identification* works with thankfulness and devotion and gives power to all practices. The *Way of Methods* activates the energies of body, speech, and mind with deep breathing techniques. It has many layered and detailed practices and a built-in progression from one level to the next. The *Way of Insight* focuses these methods primarily towards calming mind and developing its intuitive experience of non-duality. Mind may thus recognize itself either through confidence in its buddha nature, through its power, or by relying on awareness.

The broadest and closest contact with enlightenment is achieved through meditations on one's teacher as Buddha's representative.

They are used in the Way of Identification and are of major importance in the Kagyu lineage, one of the four major schools of Tibetan Buddhism. Called *Lami Naljor* in Tibetan and *Guru Yoga* in Sanskrit, the deep trust engendered in this practice allows one to include aspects from both the Way of Methods and the Way of Insight.

Whoever can apply the pure view to a human form and hold it through a many sided human exchange will soon see everything as a pure land. There is no quicker access to enlightenment. While increasingly elevating the situations of daily experience until one naturally recognizes perfection in the here and now, meditations on the teacher naturally awaken the student's beyond personal qualities. Since Buddha taught that this world is already the pure land and all beings have buddha nature, these methods are the finest that we have.

As soon as a basis of thankfulness and openness has arisen, pure focus on the teacher becomes possible. Such alchemy of experience, however, requires the utmost confidence in one's own buddha nature, meaning the certainty that highest truth is highest joy and perfection can only be recognized externally because it is the essence of one's own mind. As one solidifies the understanding that absolute truth is infinite, timeless, and everywhere, that we are all buddhas who have not yet realized it, a strong striving to remove the veils keeping the experiencer from recognizing oneself arises. The result is an all terrain, active, and unshakeable view.

While passing on his Way of Methods, Buddha transformed his body into forms of light and energy (Sanskrit: *Ishta Devata*, Tibetan: *Yidam*). Through countless and varied male and female, peace giving and protecting, enriching and fascinating buddha forms, he gave his students access to enlightening feedback, the transforming essence of his tantras. Buddhist tantras are practices that transform one's totality: body, speech and mind, weaving enlightened experiences into the very fabric of one's being. Depending on his student's wishes and abilities, they could then meditate on these forms of light, whose body positions, attributes, and colors corresponded to their own potential and were therefore attractive to them. The feedback from such buddha aspects and the vibration of their mantras activated beyond personal energy paths in the students' bodies and made their speech compassionate and wise.

Identifying with such light forms enables some to do additional work with deep breathing and ultimately use the very effective but difficult union practices in which space and bliss are inseparable. However necessary, the external conditions needed in these methods are not easily achieved, especially in the busy world today. Many of the practices can only be done in month long or year long retreats, where celibates have to meditate on imagined partners. Buddha also emanated out single forms for the students who could not yet see sexuality as pure. When giving the highest empowerments, he always transformed his own body into the united buddhas. They express oneness and total realization

Mantras provide an energy bridge to the invoked buddha forms. Each syllable in the mantra transmits specific vibrations that connect with buddha forms. They may be compared to making a phone call. They usually start with the initial OM, which is like lifting up the receiver. One is now connected to the buddhas of all times and directions. The next syllables are the number for a specific buddha and that line is never busy. The last syllable(s) give direction to the desired activity. HUNG here denotes power. HRIH invokes general compassion. DHIH offers wisdom. PE cuts through obstacles. SOHA spreads out and TAM awakens special female aspects of compassion.

Today most Westerners probably know of the most popular of Tibetan mantras, pronounced OM MANI PEME HUNG. It invokes the Bodhisattva Loving Eyes (Sanskrit: *Avalokitesvara*, Tibetan: *Chenrezig*) and activates our compassion, which is so important everywhere.

Many people use this mantra simply because it gives a good feeling, but knowing its meaning strengthens its benefit. The vibration of the syllable OM removes pride and that of MA, jealousy. NI takes away attachment. PE cuts through ignorance. ME removes greed and HUNG, making one's heart center vibrate, transforms anger.

The third method that Buddha gave to his students is the Way of Insight. Since it requires neither deep devotion nor long retreats nor hard physical exercises, as do the two approaches of identification and methods mentioned here, it is more useful in the modern world. Mind here finds a natural calm by dwelling on the breath, on an external object like a buddha statue, or on some inner state of awareness. Doing this creates focus, followed by the gradual arising of inspiration and intuition, like mud settling in a glass of water or the reflection of a mirror improving in radiance and power of reflection while being polished. When it dawns on a meditator that everything is interconnected and parts of the same totality, one is not separate from the object and act of meditation and one tastes perfection.

As mentioned above, space is inseparable from joy in the Way of Methods or from wisdom in the Way of Insight. The most effective method, if possible, is the Way of Identification, where one melts together with the teacher as all encompassing space and experiences boundless bliss. All three methods become possible due to beings' inherent buddha nature and eventually lead to full enlightenment, Mahamudra, the state of the Great Seal. Working from this highest level, Buddha shared his realization so simply and directly that there was no place for doubt, and very few who heard it could forget.

In precise instructions, Buddha let his students share the unlimited freedom in which the seeing, the seer, and the object seen are inseparably one. From then until today, this realization changes anyone who experiences it. Whenever this happens, one's mental processes become smoother and more effortless, a timeless happiness spreads, and one feels at home in every situation. Afterwards, mind's self-liberating power continues to work subliminally, constantly transforming obstacles into opportunities. It is just a matter of view, meditation, and accepting joy that enables the last veil to fall from mind.

Ever since the early 1970's, the Diamond Way lay Buddhist centers of the Karma Kagyu lineage have been developing Western access to Buddha's highest teachings. Places where lay Buddhists teach, learn and meet regularly for meditation, these centers welcome those who are interested.

In the West today, Buddhism grows under conditions similar to those during the second and successful spreading in Tibet 950 years ago. We now translate the Tibetan language into ours in the same way they once translated the Indian manuscripts into Tibetan. Buddha's teachings are often compared to a crystal, reflecting the

Diamond Way Methods
The Way of Methods, the Way of Identification and the Way of Insight

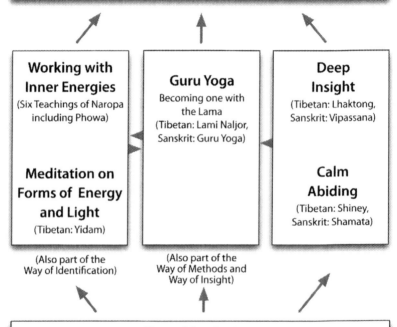

Common Goal: Realization and Highest View
in one Step or on the Four Levels of the Great Seal:
One-Pointedness, Simplicity, One-Taste, Non-Meditation

Working with Inner Energies
(Six Teachings of Naropa including Phowa)

Meditation on Forms of Energy and Light
(Tibetan: Yidam)

(Also part of the Way of Identification)

Guru Yoga
Becoming one with the Lama
(Tibetan: Lami Naljor, Sanskrit: Guru Yoga)

(Also part of the Way of Methods and Way of Insight)

Deep Insight
(Tibetan: Lhaktong, Sanskrit: Vipassana)

Calm Abiding
(Tibetan: Shiney, Sanskrit: Shamata)

Shared Beginning:
Four Basic Thoughts, Bodhisattva Attitude, Refuge,
and the Four Preliminary Practices

Way of Methods
(from Naropa to Marpa)

Way of Trust

Way of Insight
(from Maitripa to Marpa)

color of its background through facets, without changing itself.

I find it a source of increasing joy that a free and critical Western education proves to be a first class foundation for the ultimate teachings of the Diamond Way. This means that today, Buddha's highest wisdom is coming into the hands of the world's most idealistic and independent people. If we can fathom its inner richness with a minimum of restrictions, leaving monastic celibacy and elaborate traditional rituals a choice for those who want them, if we can avoid the prisons of Tibetan politics, or creating hierarchal pecking orders, many can immediately incorporate much of the teachings into their lives. Teachers of Diamond Way Buddhism are therefore responsible for the purity and relevance of its transmission. All its representatives should understand and visibly live the highest view.

Only being a conscious and responsible example ensures that something meaningful is transmitted. Being a Buddhist, with an attitude like this means to celebrate fearlessness, self arising joy, and active love. There is no finer way to thank Buddha and no more useful way to help others, than to joyfully do one's best.

Over the years an increasing number of my students have become professors of Tibetan language and "Buddhology" at various universities. Such theoretical knowledge, however, functions best when coupled with meditation. Then it touches peoples' whole being and brings maturity. In contrast to purely intellectual understanding, which can produce pride and rarely touches one's totality, meditation enables beings to live, die, and be reborn better. The ultimate practice is the joyful self-liberating action of living the Great Seal.

The now well known practice of *Phowa* is a major agent of such deep maturation. Brought to Tibet about 1,250 years ago as part of the Way of Methods, it is a uniquely useful meditation that prepares one to die consciously. It is also a very convincing example of the direct and fast benefit that may be gained from Diamond Way Buddhism.

During an intensive five day course in an undisturbed environment, my students practice the preliminary stages of death and thereby lose their fear of dying. With the outer sign of perfection from this practice and a few yearly practice sessions, one will reach the liberating mental field of the red Buddha of Limitless Light while dying. In 1987, my teachers asked me to pass on this meditation to my students, even when they have not been able to follow the gradual steps that traditionally lead to this kind of practice. Because traditional preparation usually takes years of meditation and people might die at any moment, this advice has definitely been a great gift to many.

Since 1987, about 80,000 friends worldwide have practiced the meditation in twelve to thirteen annual courses, often with thousands attending, especially in Central Europe and Russia. The Tibetans are actually amazed by the intensity of our practice and the clarity of the signs obtained. Many who thought that one had to live under difficult conditions or in distant lands to benefit from the Diamond Way have happily changed their minds.

At the time of his death Buddha was deeply satisfied with his work. He had given what people need for their enlightenment. His last advice was to not just believe his words but to examine them and trust in one's critical mind. This makes Buddha's teachings a precious and dogma free gift for independent thinking beings.

Goals of Buddha's Ways — Liberation and Enlightenment

Goal of the Small Way — Liberation

Liberation appears from removing the illusion of any existing or real self. It is the recognition that there is nothing permanent in the body, only innumerable particles whirling about. The same is true for thoughts, feelings, and mental states of one's consciousness. Although experiences might feel real as they occur, they are actually only constantly changing streams of impressions, held together by the illusion of being somehow separate and lasting.

If there is no *I,* then who can be harmed? With the knowledge that there is no real self, one's time as a target is definitively over, since there is no longer anybody to attack. When pain and other difficulties are encountered in life, *I suffer* automatically changes into the general observation, *there exists suffering.* When such insight into impermanence is experienced, it will mature and increasingly influence one's view of life until it becomes a lasting experience.

Here the meaning of the often misunderstood Small Nirvana, which translates literally as *blowing out,* becomes clear. In the schools of Hinayana Buddhism, in Ceylon and Indochina minus Vietnam, one recognizes that one may clear away any objects of consciousness as well as the idea of an independent self. It is the opposite of the state of *samsara,* where beings are stuck in the coming and going of the conditioned world. The southern schools of Buddhism are therefore satisfied with the insight that there is no self. It leads to the desired state of liberation, the end of one's own pain through the uprooting of all disturbing emotions. Then there will be no more rebirths into conditioned worlds.

The Great Nirvana of Northern Buddhism, found roughly from the Himalayas and North and Central Asia, as well as the Chinese world, aims for the realization that also the outer world is an illusion, a collective dream created from beings' condensed karmas.

Removing this second veil means full enlightenment and brings forth all of mind's unlimited powers. With that wide and brave motivation, the great voyage to enlightenment for the good of everyone begins, the Bodhisattva Way. In the highest all encompassing view of the Diamond Way, everything is mind.

In samsara, the wheel of existence, one sees the pictures. The Small Nirvana shows one the mirror. Diamond Way shows the picture and the mirror to be mutually dependent.

Goal of the Great and Diamond Ways — Enlightenment

As already mentioned, whoever wants to benefit others should neither aim for, nor stop at liberation, but gladly accept its signs as gifts on one's way to mind's full functioning. Right from the beginning, one's focus should be on reaching full enlightenment for the benefit of all. One then recognizes that all beings strive for happiness and at the same time notices their frequently dismal results. Since something absolutely bad must self-destruct, a mega turbo devil clearly cannot be the cause for such poor outcomes. Therefore beings' disturbing emotions and false concepts must be the cause and makes them material with which one can work.

Achieving the certainty that awareness, being in essence space, can in no way be harmed is the basis for the complete unfolding of mind's possibilities. Then fearless intuition, self-arising joy, and powerful active love will manifest effortlessly. They are mind's timeless essences and automatically appear with the removal of its veil of dualistic concepts. When one accomplishes this awareness one realizes the spontaneous and all knowing state of ultimate enlightenment, the Great Nirvana. With this realization, whatever happens is perceived as richness and delight. If nothing appears, mind recognizes this state as potential. If things do occur, difficult or pleasant, it is mind's free play. The fact that both can be there together, the experiencer and its objects, is mind's limitless expression.

It takes years of endeavour before one has enduring or even frequent experiences of mind's radiant space. What sees through one's eyes and hears through one's ears is an elusive customer! But there exists no other way to fulfilment and lasting happiness. At this level everything outer as well as inner emerges, plays in mind's space, is recognized through its awareness, and dissolves again in its boundlessness.

Buddhist teachers pointedly ask their students whether inner experience and outer worlds are the same as mind, or whether they are different from it. The best answer is both. Though experienced as different, all things arise and unfold in mind, are experienced through it, and dissolve back into it. They are like ocean waves. Are these waves the ocean or are they something else? Whoever recognizes this will not limit most experiences with concepts, but will simply let the timeless wisdom of body, speech, and mind hold sway. One is then neither disturbed by anything that comes up, nor sleepy and confused when nothing happens. The awareness of here and now polishes mind's mirror and brings forth its radiant power and unlimited possibilities.

As already mentioned, the removal of mind's veils inevitably leads to courage, joy, and active kindness, to minds timeless essence. The understanding that one is neither the body that decays nor constantly changing emotions but rather indestructible awareness that is like space, open and all containing, effectively uproots all fear. What can harm it? What can make space suffer?

Beyond fear, the immense richness of appearances becomes the play of mind's possibilities. Whether it manifests birth or death, coming or going, everything shows its abundance and potential. Finally, the experience of mind's limitless quality leads to skillful love. Having gained mature insight, one acts for the lasting benefit of others, undisturbed by the passing fads of time.

On this level the message is clear: Do not confine your life through guilt. Mind's essence can neither be improved nor harmed and whatever thoughts and feelings may appear simply manifest it's many sided power of expression. What is important is where these impressions arise and what perceives them. What matters is the ocean underneath the waves, the mirror in which pictures appear, the consciousness that stays essentially pure regardless of what it reflects or brings forth.

Materialistic thoughts are not a sign that one's meditation is useless. One can simply see them as practical. Nihilistic thoughts do not mean that one is a reincarnation of Nietzsche. One can just recognize that such thoughts are possible. Existential experiences prove nothing and idealistic states of mind may be enjoyed without attachment. Even the ideas about better or worse gods that have come and gone throughout history only mean that people like to project their mixed mental states into such lofty forms. Whatever appears in mind only affirms its richness, potential, and power. Highest wisdom is always highest joy and functioning, so be pleasantly surprised when such states unfold. It is only beyond hope and fear that enlightened awareness emerges and plays effortlessly.

Buddha's Conditioned and Ultimate Teachings

In monasteries and libraries that possess the Tibetan Kangyur, Buddha's 84,000 teachings are categorized into four groups of 21,000, according to their content. Their goal is always the same, to benefit beings in their lives. The first group is called *Vinaya*. Buddha gave such advice and his outer vows for individual liberation to different groups on various occasions, as advice for reasonable behavior and lifestyles that avoid attachment. In their totality there are 350 promises for nuns, 254 for monks, and 37 for novices. Lay people can make up to eight such promises of which three to five are reasonable for most today.

If one follows the advice that makes sense to oneself, one is protected from a lot of self induced suffering. Some general rules of individual behavior are useful for everyone. They include not to intentionally kill, steal, lie, harm others, lose face by getting intoxicated in a stupid way, and not to bring sexual pain to others nor play with their emotions. Such promises help people to get less caught up in the conditioned world and avoid getting such karmas back later.

The second group of teachings, called *Sutra,* are mainly meditation instructions. They were given to dismantle anger and aversion and build up compassion. They are especially helpful for lay people who have to protect loved ones, businesses, and societies with a minimum of disturbing emotions. For this purpose, both suggestions for life and meditation are given in the Sutra.

The *Abhidharma*, the third category of teachings, is for those most fortunate people who possess the ability for abstract thinking and an education permitting a philosophical worldview. Here Buddha shows how one may think logically but not what one should think, thus enabling all us to remove the roots of confusion and unclear thinking.

The methods for absorbing these first three types of teachings are similar to learning in school. What will at length be understood sinks only gradually from the head to one's heart, slowly moving from concept to experience. One still builds one's house from the ground up. Tibetans usually collect these three teachings under the general heading of Sutra (Tibetan: *Do*). It means a guiding thread showing the way.

Tantrayana (Sanskrit) is the fourth category of teachings in this classical division and means weaving or continuity. It refers to a total experience that becomes an indivisible part of oneself. The aim here is to quickly erect a house of enlightenment with the crane of highest view, in other words, to behave like a buddha until one has become a buddha.

Buddha's teachings on the tantric level always encompass body, speech, and mind, transforming views and ideas, working with breathing techniques, sexuality, and vibrations. When talking about these methods, their full name *Buddhist Tantra* should be used. This is because the Hindus use the same term, tantra, for entirely different teachings with other practices and goals. From a non-practitioner's point of view and at first glance, many images and sayings of both fine teachings seem to be similar. In fact, the ways and goals of these two traditions are different even though they both use some same symbols, such as the position of hands and most healthy figures in sexual union. A Hindu's ultimate goal is will power (Sankrit: *Shakti*). Buddhists, on the other hand, wish to discover ultimate wisdom (Sanskrit: *Jnana*, Tibetan: *Yeshe*). Also the Hindu meditator's inner energy channel lies in his spine and the Buddhist tantras work with the magnetic axis through the center of the body between the crown of the head and the g-spot or the prostate. Whoever mixes up these secret teachings will as the Tibetans say, get a head like a watermelon, full of dispersed ideas and a heart like a hazelnut, small and hard.

In the Kagyu lineage, tantra is the energy practice of the Diamond Way. It touches one's full being. It can be compared to taking a fast motorcycle down a curvy road, experiencing a free fall when skydiving, or delving into the depths of inspiration and love. It transforms humans and awakens their inherent power. The use of its most effective methods, like the practice of Conscious Dying (*Phowa*), has opened the pure lands, from which there is no falling down, to countless people over thousands of years and has brought many to enlightenment in one lifetime.

Fine lamas from the old Nyingma school debate whether their ultimate teachings of view called *Dzogchen* (Tibetan), *Maha Ati* (Sanskrit), or Great Perfection belong to Buddha's original tantra or if it represents a separate system. Both viewpoints seem legitimate. In the Karma Kagyu Diamond Way, however, the Great Seal, *Mahamudra*, shows the basis, directs the way, and is in itself, the goal of any absolute practice.

Heaven and hell happen in one's own mind. The correct understanding and application of the Diamond Way make beings great. It keeps the poor concept of *either/or* on the conditioned level where it belongs. Instead the great view of *both/and* is practical and empowers, ever more strongly, mind's true richness. Here the unlimited aspect of space becomes the source of all freedom, and even the way into this experience is exciting. One skillfully catches the mole of ordinary consciousness, puts contact lenses on its eyes, ties wings to its paws, glues feathers onto its tail, and sends it into the air like an eagle. Beyond any limitation, everything outer and inner is then constantly fresh and new.

TAKING THE
BUDDHIST PATH

APPLYING THE TEACHINGS TO LIFE

Significance of the Teacher

Nothing can replace the personal teacher-student relationship for quick learning and transformation, even in our time of internet, group work, and crash courses. With experiences and insights being transmitted holistically, the connection between a teacher and student is especially important. When a realized teacher shares his world of experience with an inspired student, he can enrich the latter directly, on conscious and subconscious levels.

Even though his teachings were preserved in the Kangyur, Buddha's most direct transmissions reach today's world in the flesh and blood of great human beings. They have practiced, embodied, and passed down his living experience from his time until now. What Buddha then shared with his brightest students was brought from India to Tibet around 750 AD by the fully realized Guru Rinpoche (Tibetan, Sanskrit: *Padmasambava*). Except for his hidden treasures, *termas*, these teachings were destroyed fifty years later by a Shamanist king. However, the magnificent hero, bodhisattva, and lay lama Marpa reintroduced the full Diamond Way methods to Tibet around 1050 AD. They remained protected and intact until the Chinese invaded in 1959. The four lineages of Tibetan Buddhism have a different position on the older and newer transmissions. The Nyingmas use what was saved of Guru Rinpoche's transmission, the Gelugpas use whatever texts can still be found, while the Sakyas and Kagyus use them all, the former in a stricter and more intellectual way. These immeasurably rich teachings, which point directly to mind, have been passed on in unbroken lines from teacher to student. The Kagyu school even takes its name from this practice: *Ka* means oral and *gyu* means lineage or transmission.

These ultimate teachings on mind survived the flight over the Himalayas by hundreds of Tibetan lamas in 1959. Those who survived long enough passed them on and they are today practiced by idealistic groups of accomplishers throughout the East and West. In these traditions the teacher is the most important factor in a student's development, because he or she awakens one's motivation and provides both the tools for enlightenment and the visible confirmation that it is possible. To reach this goal the teacher shows one's own mind and is beyond the personal. As Kalu Rinpoche, the first high Kagyu lama to teach in the West often said, "When you have learned everything from your lama, your mind and his mind are one."

Many life stories by famous yogis in India and Tibet confirm the usefulness of such a connection. Hannah's and my own first lama, Lopon Tsechu Rinpoche, whom we met in 1968, frequently said that Buddha also had lamas, meaning teachers. Naropa, Maitripa, Marpa, Milarepa, Rechungpa, Gampopa, and the seventeen Karmapas, up to today's Trinley Thaye Dorje, as well as fourteen Shamarpas, all gratefully claim to have matured and reached their accomplishment through the blessing of their teachers.

The Tibetans say, "You cannot see the summit of a higher mountain from a lower one." In the same way, it is often difficult to fully assess a teacher. It pays to rate him as high as any hopeful but sober evaluation will allow and see if the teacher is able to sustain true power and style. Why is this evaluation so important? Because the teacher is a mirror to one's mind. Highest joy is highest truth and until liberation one does not see the world, but rather projects one's own states of mind on whatever happens. Therefore all who have the good karma to experience a fine teacher on a high level simply confirm their own inner richness.

Sharing once again a quote from Kalu Rinpoche's wisdom, where it is taken for granted that the lama must have solid knowledge of the teachings and provide a reasonable example, "Whoever experiences the teacher as a buddha receives the blessing of a buddha. Whoever experiences him as a bodhisattva gets that kind of blessing. And whoever sees him as an ordinary person probably gets a headache."

Without devotion there would be no Diamond Way. None of its many realized ones would have appeared, not since Buddha's time in the East nor from the early 1970's onwards in the West. There is no faster way to enlightenment than identification with the perfection seen. Therefore, this openness is to be handled as the greatest but also the most dangerous gift, because a student needs abundant life experience to hold this high but practical view until full maturation. In this context it may relieve some to know that the teacher is a lama only when representing the Buddha and his teachings. So if from a feeling of responsibility the teacher speaks on contemporary subjects such as politics, where interpretations of Buddha's prophesies 2,500 years ago either don't exist or are unclear, that teacher is sharing personal insight, courage, and life experience.

Teachers certified through a lineage of direct experience like the Kagyus have methods and qualities that provide students with convincing methods for human growth. But students must still be careful and aware of the teacher they choose. Unfortunately it is everywhere possible to fall into the clenches of scheming or incapable teachers with the finest of credentials. Once somebody has a noble title, very few will be reasonable enough to publicly go against them. Astounding tales from former incarnations are no guarantee of perfection and any teacher must be tested thoroughly before making a commitment.

The following guidelines explain how to choose a Diamond Way teacher. The general basis when meeting with a potential guide towards a richer life is a promising chemistry that simply feels good. This teacher should therefore have compassion, understand one's needs, and generate necessary trust. He or she must have meditative experience and embody what is taught. It is refreshing if he can handle good jokes about himself and holy subjects. If a teacher has such surplus, evidently doing and saying the same, one can be taken seriously.

On the absolute level, fearlessness, spontaneous joy, and active compassion are the indispensable signs of realization. Since few can spend enough time in the immediate presence of a teacher to check out the unshakeable character of these achievements, activating one's intuition is helpful. Personally I found it useful to ask myself whether in ten years time, I would wish to have absorbed a lama's general feeling and essential behavior, because that is exactly what will happen. One may imagine oneself stealing horses or riding fast motorcycles with the teacher, to discover if one can build on a state of fundamental trust. At the very least, one should be as certain as possible of this before letting a teacher into one's mind on the ultimate level of how to see the world.

It is also important to meet several of his or her students to check if they are open minded, straight, joyful, and functioning well in the world, or if they are shy and defensive. Above all, one should examine whether one feels good and inspired in their company and if one can accept them on the human level. It is exactly in this sensitive realm of essential honesty that students and teacher share great responsibility, so that newcomers are not just routinely brainwashed into a way that does not fit their capabilities.

It is like everywhere else in life. Nothing is as convincing as genuine human accomplishments. Only a teacher with the above qualities can correctly transmit the enlightening teachings. The influence of a teacher who yields under pressure, avoids taking a responsible stand, or utters politically correct nothings simply to be popular, trendy, or to make things right for everyone, will disappear like a warm wind.

If Buddhist teachers act transparently and simply say and do the same thing, the qualities of their powerfields are quickly fathomed and realized. New brooms sweep better and hopefully the newly maturing Tibetan monks and devoted western lay teachers will succeed in separating medieval cultural habits and Buddhist politics from the timeless wisdom of the dharma. The openness and kindness of today's Western societies should enable them to do this with less hesitation and better than did many of the dignitaries from whom they now take the helm.

In today's sometimes confusing supply of information and rumors about well known lamas, it is important to recognize a teacher who is solid. He will not leave students unprotected or brainwash them with sweet words, but compassionately shares Buddha's timeless wisdom. If in order to be considered modern, the teacher tries to jump on the bandwagon and express the frequently undigested and changing notions of his present time, he will lose face and end up even more confused than his students. The stability of the teacher is needed because when a student has discarded dearly held, but faulty concepts about causality (karma), becoming practical and willing to work with the world as it is and not as most intellectuals think it should be; only an experienced teacher can guide this student into the absolute view.

The lama's only task is to develop his student's independence, compassion, and strength. He will celebrate their special qualities and be thankful that there is so much good to be shared. Above all, a spiritual teacher will insist that nobody's time is wasted. Not thinking of himself to be better than his students or expecting special treatments or luxuries, he will surround himself with people he can work with and learn from and avoid creating a court of groupies to serve or provide praise. Following the reasonable laws of free countries and not creating embarrassments, all activities shared with students will be for their inner growth.

As long as students keep their connection to the teacher, he remains responsible for their development. If one teaches on the highest level of direct experience and insight, one should also hold the energy field to protect students on their fastest of ways. No approach inspires students more deeply than to meet their timeless essence in the fearless mirror of their teacher's mind. With their discovery that their essence is also space and joy, everything is achieved!

Going the Way Alone

Whoever wants to make progress, with little connection to other Buddhists, needs vast maturity and must be able to precisely assess his or her own development. Although many would like to progress meaningfully with the help of books, pleasant spiritual thoughts, and possibly insights from earlier psychedelic experiences, this evidently does not work. During the exciting 1960's, experiments with consciousness expanding substances opened the hopeful West to inner experiences, but in ways that were fundamentally different from meditation. Even the most idealistic and interesting experiences based on chemicals are like burning one's money instead of using coal or oil; they spread one's awareness and condense the good impressions waiting to be enjoyed during months or years into some hours of extreme bliss. They therefore rob mind of good impressions gathered over many lives which had, at this time, culminated in a rare and pleasant birth in a humanistic society. Such consumption of mind's positive impressions leaves one badly prepared for the next incarnation. Correct meditation, on the other hand, sharpens and gathers mind. It brings about a growing experience of its inherent fearlessness, bliss, and limitless love.

Even the most independent minded should have no difficulty with Buddha's work. His teachings only free people and provide access to their inherent potential. He was certainly no autocratic or suppressive god, loved women, and had no moralistic streak. Since his methods help beings on the level of causality, motivation, and highest view, people can freely choose the teachings that best fit their needs. Recognizing mind's essence is much more difficult than learning about outer things, especially without friend sharing one's search. Invariably there are enemies lurking, often shades of spiritual pride and envy, which may throw a solitary practitioner off track.

Whoever decides to progress on one's own, in spite of such considerations, should not forget one essential point: The goal of all Buddha's teachings is to experience mind's timeless and naked awareness. These methods encompass three areas useful for life: activity, motivation and view. In the area of activity one learns to avoid feelings, words, and actions that result in pain. This removes the causes for later suffering and remains a sure foundation for good experiences, especially during future lives. In the second area of motivation, one develops compassion and liberating wisdom in the best possible balance. What is needed on this level is the deep wish for the happiness of all beings and an awakened ability to perceive that all phenomena, the world, others, and oneself are conditioned, constantly changing, and composite. This removes any illusion of a lasting separate or real ego and gives the freedom not to take whatever happens personally. In the third and absolute area of view, everything is inspiration. One behaves like a buddha until becoming one.

The first two areas are gradual and relatively stable. Depending on people's maturity, the first is totally and the second is partially attainable from books, alone and without a teacher. Though their goals are different, liberation or full enlightenment, a deepening observation of life and the right information may suffice to produce one approach through either understanding or motivation. However, this is not the case with the third type of teachings. The Diamond Way is vulnerable and dependent upon experience, requiring holders to pass on the teachings directly to students. Without this exchange the Diamond Way disappears, is not approachable, or is impossible to use. The methods simply do not take effect without an exchange with the lama or interaction with the centers, which represent the lineage and its powerfield. Those who dabble in the highly interesting psychology and imagery of the tantric texts, but lack devotion, will end up confused. No matter how well read they may otherwise be, head without body is not complete. Because of the lurking feeling that they are missing the real parts, they will develop a cold and intellectual kind of pride, which is rarely brought to light and worked out. Easily becoming useless in everyday life, they nourish their egos and make themselves lonely, missing the joy of mind's richness and of helping others in practical ways.

Though such potential faults must be mentioned, if people wish to practice without the worldly mirrors of their groups or teachers, the above should not be seen as an absolute *no* for mature people to pursue parts of the way alone. Much can be done, also on your own, if handled in the right way. Never before have so many gifted, independent, and idealistic humans had such a seamless access to such an array of Buddhist teachings as today, especially through books, the Internet, and other new means of communication. Due to our abstract thinking and high level of education such knowledge may even include direct teachings on mind that were very difficult to get in Tibet, though the three Red Hat schools taught them whenever possible. In such cases, life experience is all deciding, but one still needs a responsible teacher.

Until recently most available spiritual books were an unclear mix of anything exotic and New Age. Only experienced teachers and their well trained groups could cut through such confusion effectively, protecting mental health, and saving precious time. But these warnings to solitary practitioners are not the only possible cautions. Once well embarked on an established road to enlightenment, there still lurk two misleading exits on the highway to enlightenment that are not easily recognized if one does not share growth with a group. The first is a non-discriminating approach to the soft sciences, a seductive but dangerous exit. Of course, after becoming Buddhist it makes sense to continue the use of skills like healing powers and a knowledge of astrology, at least as long as they are interesting and can be directed into a Buddhist context without confusing one's meditation or view. But if in the process one forgets the ultimate goal, enlightenment for the benefit of all, a most precious opportunity is wasted and may not be found again for lifetimes.

The second slippery exit is the targeted attachment to warmly welcomed experiences. Holding on to them or hoping for them to return can seriously block a person's development and, above all, scare bright people away. Because all experiences are unfathomable and unsteady, the wish to repeat them always ultimately leads to discouragement. Trying to carry along the milestones of the past and living in what once was not only mentally develops arms like a gorilla, but the habit blocks any progress. One is then left with only a few supernatural stories, which everyone has already heard. They will not bring one to the effortless state in which mind's full potential unfolds spontaneously, the ultimate goal. It is thus wiser to enjoy the richness of the here and now than to try to repeat, prove, or hold onto past experiences. Enlightenment only arises from a relaxed state and in the fullness of space everything appears at the right time and place. Whoever simply continues along the motorway with trust in the moment will marvel at mind's boundless playfulness.

Buddhist Lifestyles

Tibetans, especially those of the three old unreformed Red Hat schools, use three practical and life oriented approaches to Buddha's teachings: those of accomplishers (Sanskrit: *Yogi*), monks, and lay people. Today most Buddhist cultures, like the Chinese, know only the latter two, which freezes their range of experience and robs their expression of much magic and human touch. They are the classes of the mostly celibate monks performing rituals and of their lay supporters. Living transmissions, however, best take place in informal situations and among yogis. Embracing all of life, such empowerments may be less moralistic, ritualistic, or organized than the monastic transmission but because they happen in every day life, their scope is broad, has a living reference, and is truly transforming. Since Buddha's time such conditions have kept his Diamond Way teachings powerful and direct. The freshest Western minds today will put up with nothing less.

For centuries in Tibet and other Buddhist countries, the monks and nuns lived separately from society and one another. They were protected by monasteries and followed strict rules of conduct. As might be expected, they were defenseless and at the mercy of internal and external politics. Everywhere at that time the lay people cared for their families and communities and also supported the spiritual life, mainly by farming. People were poorly educated and quite superstitious, but whenever possible they tried to develop devotion and apply whatever teachings they had to their everyday lives. The yogis lived outside society's norms, often in caves and with changing partners. They used every experience and enticement for getting to know their mind. Famous examples are the great yogis and realized teachers Milarepa[1] and Drukpa Kunleg.[2]

Milarepa was famous throughout Tibet for his wisdom songs. In his youth, at his mother's insistence, he invoked negative forces to kill thirty five enemies of his family. Then struck by a disturbed conscience, he found his teacher Marpa and toiled for him for many years, until at age forty four Milarepa was put on the Diamond Way. During the following thirty years he lived in caves, mainly around Mount Everest, sustaining himself mostly on a broth from stinging nettles. Increasingly his absolute view and the effective methods given by Marpa proved both his ego and the outer world to be illusory. From that point onwards he no longer had any tightness or fear. He perceived whatever thoughts arose as mind's rich play and equally enjoyed their dissolution when he gave them no attention.

In addition to teaching 5,000 female partners union meditations, the Bhutanese Drukpa Kunleg became famous for continually confronting the bourgeois morality of his time. Above all he joyfully unravelled and exposed people's pretentiousness, freeing many from their social games and rigid behavior. He unmasked hypocritical teachers and revealed those who were more interested in fame and their students' gifts, rather than the students themselves and their growth. Many of his consorts developed quickly in their shared awareness field, using the meditations that he taught them. The miracles he performed are still the folklore of Bhutan. In this stunning Himalayan kingdom he is still revered today for his realization and wish fulfilling powerfields. Varying but unmistakeable symbols of his noble male tool protect cars from accidents and bless even the holiest of monasteries.

Since in free and developed countries today people may choose the number of their offspring, there will not be any large monasteries in the West. In earlier times however, women and men who wanted to be free of family concerns had to live separately. This was not because Buddha's teachings were hostile to the body, which on the highest level is seen as a mandala of light, the male part being a diamond and the female a lotus flower. It was simply because at that time one could not make love without having children, which, in times without kindergartens, schools, and health care seriously reduced one's time for study and meditation. Though monasteries and Buddha's rules for harmoniously living in them attract far fewer people today, such constricted outer circumstances still make sense to people of some dispositions. As Buddha himself gave them these hundreds of practical outer vows, they cannot be changed. They are their protection against a confused outer world.

However, in regard to the inner promises taken by the lay people and the secret ones by the yogis, the differences in dress, lifestyle, and view so clearly marked in traditional societies disappear in the educated West today. In Tibet where yogis competed with organized red robed monks and nuns for material support from the productive working population, they needed to stand out from the general public to be noticed. Thus they gravitated towards unkempt hair, long nails, exciting behavior, and wearing cheap, uncolored cotton or wool. Such outer signs are no longer necessary. As lay people in civilized countries are educated, communicate with the world through the modern media, and no longer need hordes of children in the hope that at least some may take care of them in their old age, they gain impressions and time for inner development. Since matted hair, exotic clothing, and eccentric behavior can now be enjoyed at rock concerts and anyway only impress a few, very little keeps yogis and lay Buddhists separate.

My Diamond Way students worldwide convincingly unite the lay person's motivation of bringing benefit with the yogi's highest view. On the outer level, they lead meaningful lives in the world, dealing with everyday situations as usefully and wisely as possible. At the same time, they hold the long term benefit of all as their goal. Secretly, their view is the beyond dualistic one of the Great Seal. Being essentially yogis, they learn about their minds in and through everything that happens.

2,500 years ago in India, there was little awareness in society of manipulating people. Therefore, most people welcomed Buddha's practical advice on cause and effect as simply helpful. Aiming for all to live better and with ultimate values, some focused on his teachings of wisdom and compassion and enjoyed a rich inner life. But a select handful at Vaishali and elsewhere, like King Indrabodhi, had perfected enough of the pure view to be given the ultimate methods of the Diamond Way.

Today in our Western countries, with such advanced levels of independence and education brought about by so much good karma, conditions are different. At least among my students, most are inspired by the highest view. They immediately want to experience mind's space as joy. As our social systems function, the search for wisdom and compassion, the components of a rich inner life, now usually finds expression through philosophy and psychology and may attract a similar percentage of our population as at Buddha's time. Finally, when countries degenerate into over administered nanny states, most people naturally abdicate responsibilities for their behavior and leave the fine print concerning cause and effect to the bureaucracy and police. People then tend to think if one is not caught, then things must be okay.

Whoever works for the full realization of all beings using specific situations and capabilities of students continues Buddha's transmission in an unbroken flow. This can happen in meditation centers where idealists take on public responsibilities and help as supporters and protectors or work as traveling or local Buddhist teachers. Each of these activities is good. Being living examples to family and friends is actually how most practitioners benefit others best and also come to trust their own potential most deeply.

If in addition, the causes of people's difficulties are resolved, if they experience the effect and structure of Buddha's countless methods, people's confidence in way and goal must naturally grow. A teacher may then stabilize and round off the levels of development that people have already reached and offer them a joyful anticipation of the next steps. In order to have quick and far reaching changes happen in people's actual lives, however, the classical division of Buddha's teachings into the text groups of Vinaya, Sutra, Abhidharma and Tantra can only be a theoretical guide. It remains conceptual and does not touch one's whole being. The following total access to the house of Buddha's teachings, consisting of three pillars and three levels under the roof of highest insight, goes much deeper and gives a practical overview.

THE HOUSE OF BUDDHA'S TEACHINGS

At the beginning of one's spiritual development, regardless of how many lives or world cycles ago that may have started, beings basically aim for their own benefit. Gradually, experience and increased intelligence show them that such results can only emerge through meaningful thoughts, words, and actions. Thus conscious activity begins on the level of cause and effect and one thereby enters the Small Way, the outer teachings that consolidate everything. Because mind has found peace, the liberating wisdom of non-ego appears, the goal of Southern Buddhism or the Small Way.

Here mind understands that there can be no lasting me or self, either in one's changing body or in one's transient feelings, and with that recognition one is no longer vulnerable. From this secure basis the dreamlike quality of the outer world is noticed. As the limitlessness of beings and their wishes for happiness are further recognized, a motivation is born to explore all aspects of mind and the world for the benefit of all. Thus compassion, inspired wisdom, and mind's inherent search for perfection provide entry into a full but gradual development. One is now able to work with the inspiring means of the Great Way.

From here one's logic and compassion clearly show that to be absolute, truth must be timeless and everywhere. One can only recognize it in a buddha or lama outside oneself because this truth is already inherent in one's mind. All have buddha nature. It is space and awareness inseparable, but this is an understanding one needs to discover. This insight opens all doors to the view and methods of the Diamond Way, Buddha's ultimate and secret third level of directly knowing mind. Its ability to identify with enlightenment is the most perfect and exciting of methods.

Each of these three levels of development corresponds to a specific human type: the self-centered, the altruist, and the accomplisher or yogi. They are like the rungs on a ladder; each further step is only reachable by passing the former. Each level contains necessary information that can be debated, meditations to internalize the teachings, and a supportive lifestyle. (See diagram page 90). If a high level of teaching immediately makes sense to one in this life, its foundation was probably established in an earlier existence, but it is still advisable to periodically check the underlying structure. Since the countless sensory distractions while being in a body seriously limit and slow down mind's free play, one's inherent wisdom must be reawakened in each new life, and consciously kept fresh. This calls for training one's awareness concerning one's body, speech, and mind, until red lights flash automatically before mistakes are made. This is best done by establishing solid pillars of proven information, daily habits of meditation, even if short, and behaviors fit for holding and deepening what is realized during daily life.

View − Meditation − Action

The first pillar must be knowledge and view. Whichever level one hopes to perfect, one must first know its way and goal. Instructions here should be concrete, close to real life, understandable, problem solving, and effective. A student's courage and willingness are also indispensable for checking out what is imparted, unfettered by any fear or dogma. Whether one is looking for an unchallenged everyday existence, a rich inner life, or the experience of being a buddha among buddhas, these levels of knowledge and examination are necessary.

Buddha's very last words show that he wanted his students to critically examine teachings and teachers for themselves. After his saying that he could "die happily because he had already passed on what may benefit beings," Buddha added two last points that make his teaching the only choice for many today: "Now, don't believe anything just because a buddha told you. Check out everything for yourselves. See if the teachings fit your own experiences," and, "Be your own guiding lights." That is why one must not make dogmas out of any relative advice that Buddha gave. They are steps on the way. Only the absolute wisdom teachings concerning mind's essence, the emptiness of anything outer or inner, and buddha nature are on the level of absolute reality.

Also, if science should contradict certain details in the Buddha's teachings, one should always follow science's proven knowledge. As far as I can see, for a Buddhist this is easy to do. The most recent scientific discoveries evidently come ever closer to Buddha's view of things, including the nature of matter and the possibilities of countless big bangs and parallel universes. For Buddha and his students, no religion that enforces or dictates anything criminal or claims to stand above what is humane is acceptable. Knowing the distinction between relative personal experiences of phenomena and the happiness or pain they produce and their absolute, blissful, and dreamlike empty essence is essential here.

Meditation is the central pillar of Buddha's teachings. It takes what is learned and understood intellectually in one's head and moves it to the heart, making it a part of one's life. Allowing for distance to one's daily mind flow, the recognition of the impermanence of any obstacle permits spontaneous insights to arise, along with blissful and enlightening states of deep understanding. When one's awareness of the emptiness of any lasting personal nature and the mutually conditioned character of all outer and inner appearances becomes stable, the rest is a pure gift.

From this point on, mind effortlessly brings forth its most original and enlightened qualities. Thus spontaneously co-emergent wisdom, essential fearlessness, self-arising joy, and active compassion become one's life. One is nakedly present in the here and now and everything around has the taste of growth and absolute meaning. As meditation activates mind's timeless force and joy, then fear, clinging and ill will disappear. Like a glass of murky water settling and becoming transparent, mind's awareness reveals the true nature of whatever occurs. Thus total certainty arises about how things are.

The third pillar, action, grounds and protects what was already attained. The life experience it produces is essential and not just for oneself. Nothing is less convincing than the stiff and self protective behavior that arises from a lack of maturity or the wobbly emotional states caused by lack of experience. It is therefore essential that any achievement in meditation be tested and solidified in the world. With no real certainty grounding one's insights, mind is mutable and one is not reliable.

On all three levels, the pillar of holding and expanding one's maturity helps the practitioner avoid disturbing feelings and harmful behavior. Thus one develops inwardly and for the good of all, enabling everyone to reach the highest view. The totality of Buddha's teachings may thus be imagined as a building with three pillars, each with three levels, and the ultimate insight of the Great Seal as its roof. They were given to provide everyone with a correct understanding of their potential, the appropriate methods for realizing it, and real staying power to not lose it again.

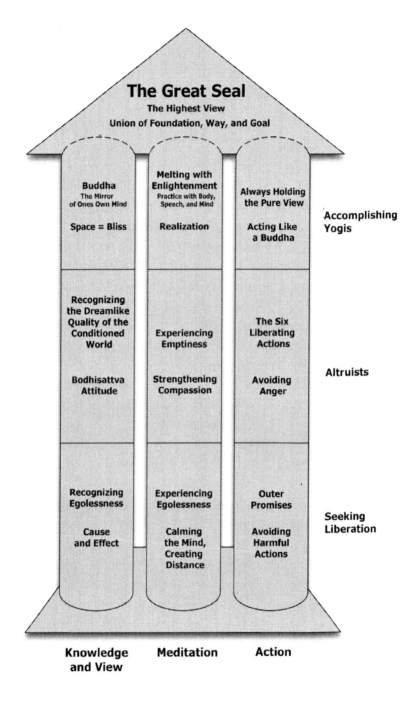

The Great Seal
The Highest View
Union of Foundation, Way, and Goal

Buddha
The Mirror
of Ones Own Mind

Space = Bliss

Melting with Enlightenment
Practice with Body,
Speech, and Mind

Realization

Always Holding the Pure View

Acting Like a Buddha

Accomplishing Yogis

Recognizing the Dreamlike Quality of the Conditioned World

Bodhisattva Attitude

Experiencing Emptiness

Strengthening Compassion

The Six Liberating Actions

Avoiding Anger

Altruists

Recognizing Egolessness

Cause and Effect

Experiencing Egolessness

Calming the Mind, Creating Distance

Outer Promises

Avoiding Harmful Actions

Seeking Liberation

Knowledge and View

Meditation

Action

Overcoming One's Suffering —
The Level of Seeking One's Own Liberation

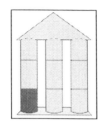

Knowledge and View:
Recognizing Egolessness

People who primarily seek their own benefit and protection need teachings on cause and effect on the worldly outer level. Since yesterday's thoughts become today's words and may easily become tomorrow's action, one's mental state is highly important. On this level Buddha taught about what brings trouble and how to turn body, speech, and mind away from harm. The emphasis was then on the activities that one would do well to avoid. To modern Westerners, this material often appears moralistic or dry, since everyone in our overly regulated societies already has enough prohibitions to circumvent.

Buddha's aim with any class of instructions was to help people understand their situation, be less distracted and better able to focus on meditation, thus giving them more meaningful lives on a lasting basis. He never wanted followers but delighted in training future colleagues. Today Buddha's methods are particularly attractive to independent minds.

To obtain the lasting basis which appears from feeling secure, Buddha made the realization of non-ego the main focus of his foundational Small Way, today called The Way of the Elders of the Order or Southern Buddhism. Taking his students with a more self-centered disposition on the path of utmost and exact investigations of both body and mind, he had them research whether anything at all could be found that was constant, existent, or personal that could therefore be called a *self*. After such attempts failed repeatedly, his students' certainty saw that if there was no self, one could also not be a target. As there was nothing personal to constitute a lasting and vulnerable entity, there was nothing to worry about. The resultant state of liberation causes one to be unshakable and is the goal on the Small Way.

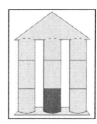

Meditation: Calming, Holding, and Recognizing Mind

Meditation turns one's well tested and correctly understood knowledge into experience. On Buddha's first level of teachings, the main methods given are those to quiet and hold mind. They create a protective distance to inner and outer disturbances. Such exercises build the basis for insight and are called *Shamata* in Sanskrit and *Shiney* in Tibetan. Their purpose is to create space between subject and object, between the meditator and one's varying experiences. Recognizing the impermanence and illusory nature of any ego trip, this practice increasingly allows one to choose whether to participate in life's tragedies or to avoid them. Most obtain this protective distance from events by focusing on one's breath or on some other object or activity of mind.

As the waves of impressions come to rest and the aware space between them grows, liberating insight emerges. The beyond dual state that appears is called deep or penetrating insight, *Vipassana* in Sanskrit and *Lhaktong* in Tibetan. Whoever can hold such realization in the laboratory of their meditations will gradually accomplish the same in daily life. Shiney and Lhaktong are the basis of all Buddhist meditations, regardless of how varied and different they may appear.

Two practices to quiet mind and help gain a distance from one's emotions are the Rainbow Light meditation and the Meditation on One's Breath, found at the end of the book.

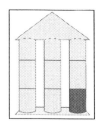

Action: Avoiding Harmful Acts — Making Outer Promises

Innumerable useful, harmful, or meaning-less actions make up everyone's life. Probably because we have ten fingers, Buddha like Moses, divided one's harmful exchange with the world into ten actions that have heavy consequences and thus are best avoided. As might be expected from Buddha, they are not commandments but logical advice from a friend. Concerning the body the promises are to avoid killing, stealing, and bringing sexual pain to others. Concerning speech they are to avoid lying to harm others, slander, coarse and offensive speech, and meaningless chatter. Concerning mind they are to avoid ill will, envy, and wrong views.

TEN HARMFUL ACTIONS

Killing always brings suffering and the impressions that accompany it weigh heavily on one's mind. Buddha warned very strongly against taking life, stating that when one is reborn as a human, the result from killing others will be a short life. Furthermore one can expect difficult future lives in unpleasant places and with many illnesses. *The Jewel Ornament of Liberation* by Gampopa[3] describes these lifetimes as being "in a desolate area in a land with all kinds of war and misfortune."

Stealing to Buddha meant to take what is not given. At his time there hardly existed common property and surviving was much harder than in today's industrialized countries. At that time people were often very poor, though not as destitute and hopeless as in the overpopulated regions around the equator today. The consequence of stealing without purifying these actions is to lose one's own possessions in this and future lives, again and again.

Causing sexual harm touches on the widest realm of human behavior. Buddha was wise to warn forcefully against incest. He also warned not to get involved in people's preferences as long as it is consensual and nobody is harmed. Sexuality depends on the cultural context, one's own tendencies, shared karmas, and personal attractions. In Greenland a host's wife may be part of the hospitality, if it is all right with her, while the Muslim tries to hide his women in tents when in public or to keep them locked up at home. Also, some people and cultures are naturally trusting and generous, while others are insecure and therefore want to control everything. It is important to pay special attention here, because there is no area of human expression with a greater variety of games and a stronger influence on people's happiness or suffering. The consequence of bringing sexual harm is future rebirths in deserts and one will experience painful relationships, both in this life and in future existences.

Lying comes in two varieties, serious and everyday untruths, big lies and little lies. Little lies like saying, "The bus was late," when one really wanted to enjoy someone's good company in bed a bit longer, counts among silly habits. These lies do not harm anyone directly but their usefulness is short lived. Buddha also indicated that people who told little lies would later have bad breath.

Serious big lies are those that aim to consciously harm others through willful deception. An example of this is when one intentionally accuses an innocent person of a criminal act. Spiritual lies, like deceiving someone about one's meditation experiences, can lead to even greater harm. This is a serious lie because the deep trust is the most liberating of human qualities and once lost, it may take many lifetimes to rebuild.

Slander should especially be avoided, because its cause is anger. To talk negatively about others behind their backs, unless they are public persons or one speaks to make others aware of a dangerous example to their own lives, means taking part in others' negativity. It also destroys friendships and splits people up. Such behavior is self-defeating. Nothing turns against oneself faster than harmful words.

Coarse and offensive speech is not only a sign of bad upbringing; it is also most unpleasant and embarrassing. It gives a cheap feeling to one's life and one will hear many bad things about oneself as a result. Even in times of peace, destructive language can reach and negatively affect many beings.

Meaningless chatter is mentioned because it is a leak in one's accumulation of good qualities. Though pleasant and relaxing in good company, one will shudder to discover how much precious time and energy this habit uses up. The hidden emotions behind the words are also not always the best. Catchy stories about others often involve a lot of jealousy or pride. As may be learned worldwide from the popular press, such feelings completely overtake basic sympathy, go beyond personal insights, and destroy good wishes. When one engages in meaningless chatter or keeps others from doing something useful with their time, the result is that others will not take one seriously.

Regarding mind's sources of disturbance, three emotions and their expressions are the most significant, because these thoughts and feelings usually have consequences leading to words and actions, solidifying habits and results.

Hate expressed as anger comes from the difficult area of ill will and should actually not be such a formidable opponent. Anyone healthy who can see how vulnerable beings are, how all seek happiness but out of ignorance behave in ways that can only lead to later suffering, should be able to develop deep compassion for them all. It makes sense to see such people as confused patients and not as enemies. If someone is consciously trying to be unpleasant, one can stop them much more effectively with a clear head than from feelings of revenge or resentment. If one allows negative attitudes to become habitual, one will lead a frustrated life filled with rejection.

Most embarrassing is when people have shared great and idealistic visions or the intimacies of love and then turn against each other. Such behavior is deeply painful and a big waste of time. In such cases one should limit one's personal expectations, rather than act against a former partner. If people separate with bad wishes, the maturing process that occurred during the relationship stops. In these cases one has actually not learned anything.

If the same problems appear with serial partners, the difficulties are really one's own anyway. Otherwise, they would not happen, one would not take them personally or label them as exotic and they would not hurt. Whoever notices a pattern of difficult feelings emerge, should know that probably the current occurrence is not the first time they have appeared and that one has had already missed opportunities to overcome them!

Envy blocks the natural flow of self-emerging richness that is the essence of space. Every kind of greed or attachment is an expression of poverty, of feeling a separation between oneself and others and shows a lack of basic trust. It is the opposite of rejoicing and one is constantly driven by demands that will never be satisfied. For example, one should not envy rich people unless it is for their generosity, which makes good karma for their future lives. Otherwise too many possessions simply make the owners into slaves of their things and rob them of their time and mental peace. After a certain point many of these people actually work full time to protect their money, hiding it from the taxman or other greedy people, and the fun of being rich is definitely over. Mind is then trapped and the owner will have the dubious final honor of leaving the problems behind for ungrateful heirs and their grateful lawyers.

Ignorance is the incessantly bubbling source of the preceding nine disturbances and is the basic cause of all suffering. It comes only from mind's inability to see itself. Neither gods nor devils are our masters. Instead this fundamental ignorance in the form of false view hides mind's essential clarity and inherent enlightenment.

However, mind also possesses the tools for its liberation, awareness, and its striving for perfection. When such qualities which reside in everyone can be activated, they lead to self-reliance and independence. And any, hopefully frequent, comparison of one's own views with Buddha's teachings shows the way out of the circle of disturbing thoughts words and actions.

As mentioned above, the key is to establish a confidence in causality. It entails understanding that the brain transforms but does not create mind, which in its essence is timeless space, and seeing mind's expression as a stream of sensory and emotional imprints held together by the illusion of an *I*. Ultimately, as perfection is reached, mind is recognized as limitless, indestructible, blissful, and kind.

Buddha advises a four step process for all who want to free their store consciousness most effectively. Called counter forces, one avoids suffering in this and future lives by:

- Regretting whatever harm one does, speaks, or thinks, causes others to do, or enjoys seeing others do.
- Wanting to free mind of negative impressions.
- Deciding not to repeat actions or behaviors that cause suffering.
- Applying intelligent and practical antidotes to transform whatever trouble actually arises.

OUTER PROMISES FOR SELF LIBERATION

Buddha gave his students the outer rules to protect them from losing their way. Their goal is to avoid thoughts, words, and actions that stand in the way of a calm mind and to help people let go of attachments. Buddha gave five promises, which are part of the Eightfold Path, that apply to lay people in today's world:

- Do not kill. Most people at that time were farmers and slaughtered their own animals. Today city dwellers can strengthen that promise.
- Do not lie to harm others or wrongly present one's own spiritual attainments.
- Do not take what is not given.
- Do not bring sexual harm to anyone.
- Do not get intoxicated.

Numerous other restrictions appeared as answers to daily events concerning his groups. There are three more rules that can be added for celibate lay people, like wearing no ornaments or sleeping in high beds, expanding into thirty seven promises for novice monks. The 254 vows for fully ordained monks and the 350 for nuns are a compilation of his vast practical advice given to help his groups of celibate students live better together. Buddha was certainly no bureaucrat. Having lived with 500 delightful consorts during his life as a young prince, he certainly had no fear of sex; therefore his words on celibacy and other topics was only to people wanting to avoid starting families and keep a simple life.

From the ultimate state one sees all phenomena as wondrous and charged with deepest meaning and feels absolutely no joy in limiting people's lives. Therefore whenever conditions forced him to add a new rule, Buddha must have exclaimed, "Why do they now get into things like that?" While the celibate monastic practitioners are bound to take and keep their whole set of vows, lay people should examine which ones they want to keep. Some lay people and yogis make such outer promises. Others do not.

Because Buddha wisely stayed out of people's bedrooms, today his students can live in and benefit the most varied cultures of the world. However, one is not without responsibility. Where women are suppressed or other criminal conditions prevail, one should take action as a citizen within the realm of what is possible.

Buddhist promises are not comparable with Christian commandments or Hindu duties, where gods want something from their customers. They are the total opposite of personal divine revenge or religious death sentences like the Muslim fatwas. No one has ever been persecuted for Buddha's sake. Nobody proselytized and no holy war was ever fought in Buddha's name, though there are causes for which Buddhists will fight. In Tibet the worst crimes committed were ones of omission and due to the misunderstanding that karma means fate or destiny that makes people passive. Karma actually means causality and whatever hasn't happened yet can be changed. Due to this misconception, the power hungry politicians who controlled Central Tibet continued to employ gruesome medieval punishments. These were, however, the crimes of a feudal class and had nothing to do with Buddha's teachings; certainly their abuses were not ordered by any of his holy books.

Being neither tribal nor fanatical, Buddha simply wanted everyone to reach lasting happiness by knowing mind. Therefore, one needed to understand and want the promises that one made. Also, although conservative societies frown upon such acts, in Buddhism, whenever religious promises are no longer useful or even counterproductive because the benefit of others takes precedence, one should give them back before breaking them. In this case one does not lose whatever good karma one has achieved; only the future protection they afford from possibly heedless actions in the realm of human interchange.

This level of promises makes sense, because the law of cause and effect never rests. Whatever one thinks, says, or does, without changing or meditating it away before it matures, will bring about future happiness or pain, most of it after this life. The above outer promises therefore strengthen and protect.

Wisdom and Compassion for the Benefit of All — The Level of Altruists

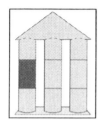

Knowledge and View: The Illusory Character of the Conditioned World

The level of cause and effect leads one to a more pleasant feedback from the surrounding world and one's own store consciousness. With such trusting disposition, additional potential traits emerge in mind. When less energy is needed for one's inner and outer entanglements the resulting excess manifests as beyond personal wisdom and wide expressions of compassion. One is then more open to the world and to beings, and everything petty and limited gradually loses its foundation.

From this level of motivation, the bodhisattva attitude influences every experience. One now wants to reach enlightenment for the good of all. Here it is sufficiently clear that one can do little for others while still confused and having difficulties oneself. One takes on one of the three expressions of compassion already mentioned: steering the world as a king, sharing experience on the way as a ferryman, or helping others first like a true friend. The perfection of these three approaches removes the separation between others and oneself.

When surplus is achieved, taking over the space from mind's disappearing veils and habits, enlightened wisdom grows. It again enhances the depth of one's empathy and two motivations radiate ever more convincingly through every new crack in one's illusory walls of disturbing emotions and stiff ideas. Thus right action arises spontaneously and without any tinge of control or taboos. For this purpose one chooses among Buddha's countless teachings, those that clearly benefit this century and the West, deciding early on to bring joy through one's body, speech, and mind. Whoever trusts his or her own abilities will have no problem with Buddha. He is clearly not a distant moralistic god, but rather one's friend and one has no need to put the richness of physical life down.

For lay people, as for yogis, it is meaningful to use one's body for the benefit of others: to protect them, give them love, and be generous. Speech brings growth through showing others both their minds and the world. It helps them understand their situation, find inner freedom, and discover how to work together. Buddha's advice here is once again common sense: to wish the best for everyone, to share in whatever good that others do, and to develop the widest possible insight. Whoever experiences the world as a dream, while simultaneously understanding its conditioned and causal nature, will inspire countless beings.

Taking his students beyond the belief in a lasting reality of things by refuting the dualistic philosophies of realism, existentialism, materialism and nihilism, Buddha conveyed the one and all encompassing view that only consciousness is timeless and everything else is in constant flux and thus really an illusion. However, there is a way to move from relative experience to ultimate perfection. Enlightenment springs from consciously producing even better dreams until mind dares to go beyond its images and identify with that awareness which knows them! Bad dreams, on the other hand, created by harmful activities and a lack of openness to people, also naturally take on reality. They limit and close down mind's overview; they make those believing in them increasingly dependent on the help or intervention of others.

Meditation: For the Benefit of All Beings

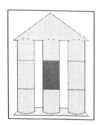

When meditating on Buddha's second level of teachings, his Great Way (Mahayana), the stakes are everybody's happiness. If enlightenment for all is one's goal, the wish for a secure mental state of calm with minimal pain lacks the power necessary for transformation. Only mind's motivation to benefit all, sharpened through one's daily observation of beings' behavior, can form a lasting foundation. Therefore this motivation is activated at the beginning and end of all Great Way meditations. Beginning with the Four Basic Thoughts which turn one's mind to lasting values, then proceeding with the Great Way refuge, which includes one's teacher or lama, the practices achieve effectiveness through a wish to reach enlightenment for the benefit of all beings.

With such motivation, the Shiney and Lhaktong practices quickly display ever finer layers of wisdom and compassion in mind. Such meditations end as they start, with sharing one's accumulated inner wealth with all beings. They teach how to train one's bodhisattva attitude until it springs forth automatically in daily life. Developed at first in a supportive atmosphere, many abilities will grow and one's example of combining compassion and skillful means will surely bring many on the same path to meaningful and lasting happiness. An example of this kind of meditation is the Meditation of Giving and Receiving, found at the end of the book.

Action: Securing a Rich Inner Life

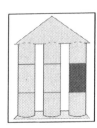

While developing compassion and wisdom, one's practice can infinitely benefit by continuously filling the mind with good impressions. They create surplus and space so that whatever happens is experienced as beyond personal. At this stage, one makes the Bodhisattva Promise that protects this most noble generous attitude and gives ultimate meaning to life. This promise consists of the *wish to go*, the desire to reach enlightenment so one can be useful to all beings. The going itself, the practical part of this promise, consists of six enlightening actions.

SIX LIBERATING ACTIONS — THE PARAMITAS

Whoever wants to succeed in life, to feel free and perhaps to hold responsibility for others will have to skirt a few constricting rules.

With nanny states encroaching ever more on people's lives and blocking their search for freedom, it is advisable to set one's own and humanistic standards in the world. For this reason, Buddha taught the way of the bodhisattvas. It supplies the motivation and necessary insight for practical people who maintain societies and have families. With this attitude they can make their everyday choices and experiences into steps towards liberation and enlightenment.

Sanskrit has the suffix *ita.* It means going or wishing, a striving that would be recognized as positive whether on Greenland or in the Congo. Buddha, however, speaks of *paramitas.* What does this prefix *param* mean? It means *trans* or that which takes one beyond. Normal kind deeds fill mind with pleasant impressions. They mature under given conditions as states of happiness, making mind confident. Mind then dares to rest in that which knows and surrounds its experiences, meaning itself.

As long as the notion persists that a real subject does something to an existing object, wonderful acts do not liberate but should still be performed. They benefit all and provide the basis for future relative happiness. To enlighten beings and bring ultimate joy, however, activity only brings freedom when combined with the insight that the doer, the thing done, and the receiver are all interdependent parts of a totality and that none of them possesses a permanent individual nature. Given that such satisfying wisdom is new to non-Buddhist cultures and in most cases will unfold only gradually, what skillful actions can best anchor them in one's life?

Buddha's first advice is **generosity.** One can see the world as a splendid hall decorated for huge celebrations. Everything is there, every richness of potential experience is present. But if nobody actively gives of their own, if no one breaks through self conscious hesitation and gets out on the dance floor, the party will never get started. When one breaks the ice and affirms one's confidence in others' fine qualities through giving, one also shows the value of what is shared. Since such acts are inspiring, others will join, pass them on, and many will benefit.

The traditional Buddhist texts mention three kinds of generosity, which are expressed according to the conditions of the times, cultures, and human capabilities involved. The first kind of generosity is giving people what they need for their survival. It benefits them for a while, but then makes them dependent. Second, one supplies education enriching people's lives and helping them take care of both themselves and others. That helps during this life. Finally one may contribute the liberating and enlightening teachings, which benefit beings during life, death, and all future lives, until enlightenment. They alone bring steady growth and lasting happiness. Pointing to mind's absolute qualities, these teachings bring forth the only feelings that are reliable: intuition, fearlessness from discovering mind to be indestructible space, joy from noticing mind's spontaneous play that creates the inner and outer worlds, and active compassion from experiencing mind's boundlessness and all beings' search for happiness.

For the 85% of humanity that lives in overpopulated countries and ghettos, poor and in misery, victims of religions that prefer uneducated quantity to quality and forbid people necessary family planning education, even the first two kinds of generosity are difficult to provide. In rich countries where many die from too much fat around the heart and cities separate people with so much glass, steel, and concrete that they can hardly get close physically, however, the most important gift on the first two levels is sufficient neighborliness, trust, time, and warmth. The ultimate gift for idealists is more evident today than ever before. Guiding others by bringing enlightening teachings to them, one really helps them grow. There exists no better tool than meaningful generosity for showing how precious others are to us.

The bonds thus generated are precious. Since they are such effective motors for growth, they should not be squandered through clumsy or harmful actions or words. For that reason Buddha's second liberating action is **meaningful behavior.** Here Buddha shows the potential of beings' three gates for useful activity. One may here employ the body positively to protect others, to give them what they lack, and for non-celibates, to give love. The task of speech is to say what is, to bring people together, to show them the world, and to guide them to meaning and joy. Finally, working skillfully with mind means wishing everything good to everyone, sharing joy in the exemplary actions that others perform, and trusting causality in one's own life.

Honest people cannot substitute the word *morality* here. Ruling classes worldwide always use this term to keep more vulnerable classes in line and under control. For example, in Europe for over a thousand years, church and state have worked seamlessly together, filling their pockets and blocking the creativity of highly capable populations. Through teachings on morality, whoever the state did not catch during this life, the church promised to send to hell afterwards.

It is always dangerous to use one single word, morality, to describe such a wide range of lifestyles and behavior. It can be manipulated much too easily. To encourage people to reflect before making knee jerk judgments about others and to activate their life experience, Buddhists prefer expressions like useful activity, intelligent comportment, circumspective action, and meaningful behavior. And while Buddha's ten pieces of advice for the Small Way focus on what it is better not to do, say, and think, the mindset of his students on the Great Way calls for a positive approach to causality.

The third liberating action, **patience**, preserves accumulated good energies. Qualities of patience include perseverance and endurance, including going through hardships in order to learn. Since anger so massively destroys the good impressions that one builds up, Buddha calls patience angers antidote and "the most beautiful but most difficult garment one can wear."

Buddha's fourth recommendation is to develop **enthusiastic effort**, or the **joy of doing**. This means to gladly perform what brings benefit to all beings, thereby overcoming laziness. Whoever lacks such expansive diligence will become older without becoming wiser, and nothing is more directly transferred from one life to the next than one's level of activity. Therefore, it is important to go beyond one's comfort zone and habitual limits. Regardless of what one may wish to learn or achieve, it requires energy. The benefit of these four liberating actions is generally evident to anyone with life experience. Generosity brings human connections. Meaningful behavior directs them well and patience makes them firm. Enthusiastic action provides power and growth.

Meditation, the fifth of Buddha's advised actions, primarily focuses on what is meaningful and then accomplishes it. Whoever wants to solidify their realization should definitely learn it. Non-meditators can hardly stabilize their minds. They shift from one emotional track to another, often without knowing it, making them unclear and wearing them out. As brain research increasingly shows, the effects of meditation are visible, harmonious, and beneficial. Through deep absorption the imprints of useful thoughts, words, and deeds are skillfully enhanced, while the harmful ones are released. This leads to confident good feelings and trust, or insights and better behaviors following purifications. If harmful feelings take control of body and speech, we may easily destroy something expensive, say something embarrassing, loose face, or make enemies.

Alternatively striving and relaxing any expectations for results, such methods are inspired by and lead to the sixth liberating action, **wisdom**, which ultimately brings about enlightenment. Wisdom is the exquisite tool for knowing mind through the recognition of its insubstantiality and emptiness.

If ten liberating actions, *goings beyonds*, are counted, the last four are furthermore explained as **methods**, **accomplishments**, **buddha qualities**, and timeless **self-arisen wisdom**. In the texts the first five liberating actions, explained above, are often compared to strong legs. They provide the power to make one's life meaningful and to benefit all. The eyes that give them direction are the deep insights of Buddha's 84,000 teachings.

As rungs on a ladder, Buddha's Great Way proceeds from the liberating understanding of the Small Way, the non-existence of a vulnerable self or ego and continues on to enlightenment by also negating any truly existing outer world or entity. By also removing mind's second veil of concepts, the goal of mind's full potential is reached. The necessary realization on both levels is that for something to truly exist there must be some permanence, but that all things change on every level, outer as well as inner, everywhere and at all times.

Buddha expressed this truth through his well known statements, "Form is emptiness. Emptiness is form. Form and emptiness cannot be separated." This can be observed in today's scientific discoveries. Contemporary physicists in Hamburg, among them students and friends of mine, recently collided quarks, the smallest parts of the atom, sending them back into space. Shortly after this time, near San Francisco, other scientists were amazed to see particles appear in an absolute vacuum. Most fantastic of all is Professor Zeilinger, who my wife and I visited in Vienna, proved that space transfers information.

Removing stiff ideas about existence or non-existence, disturbing feelings also dissolve by the recognition of non-ego. Buddha thus frees mind to express its full potential. At this point, doing good becomes self-evident because one sees that all beings and things are interconnected and can be perfected. In addition, whatever one sets in motion will necessarily return to oneself. When one reaches this realization, it becomes natural to work harder to benefit beings.

The Bodhisattva Promise formulates and focuses one's wish to develop for the good of all. As it is an inner practice, working with motivation and logic in decision making, it especially targets anger, the most harmful among disturbing feelings, with one's most effective tools for transforming feelings and seeing events as passing dreams. The recognition that people behave the way they feel should evoke compassion. In addition, a general understanding that anger and brutality are signs of weakness and impotence is needed. The fact that powerful people give others freedom and protect them should make such roles less attractive to the deeply immature.

Buddhist tantric methods involve body, speech, and mind. They belong on the third and ultimate level of the Diamond Way and will be discussed in the next pages. For those who choose to stop at this level, it may be interesting to know that the sharp sound of PE dissipates sudden anger and that repetitions of the syllables OM MANI PEME HUNG gradually transform all disturbing feelings. Please try them out!

Until a few years ago, this Great Way aspect of Buddha's advice for transforming negative states into effective wisdom was not included in most psychological views. Still today there are certain groups that vehemently insist on their right to negativity and unhappiness. Yet if one compares adherents to this school of therapy, who are attached to assigning blame to others and caught in numberless expressions of anger, with mature practitioners of Buddhism, it becomes clear that the thick skinned Far Eastern approach is preferable.

Of course anything harmful to people should be avoided. Yet the habit of blaming others for one's own trouble is a serious mistake. It makes one feckless and weak. Whether one likes it or not, the law of cause and effect applies also to oneself. The troubles others bring now are the results of actions and conditions one created in an earlier life and did not manage to purify. Action and reaction function across relative lifetimes, and if not dissolved, whatever one puts into the world or one's own subconscious remains and continues to surface until purified.

Since something absolutely negative will eventually self destruct and cannot exist for long, Buddha explains that the root of suffering is not a devil with horns, smelling of sulfur, but basic ignorance. This powerful emotion makes one search for happiness in objects and through actions that can only bring the opposite result. Being ultimately illusory, however, negative states can be removed. Basic ignorance being their cause, a dualistic view and any moralistic pointing of fingers are meaningless. The ultimate essence of all beings is their buddha nature and although one may have created a painful potential for oneself, Diamond Way Buddhist methods and a non-dualistic view empower mind to remove whatever troubles have not yet matured.

Evolving means enjoying what is pleasant as blessings to be shared with others and experiencing anything difficult as part of the learning process and examples of mind freeing itself from faulty concepts. One's wish is that all beings may have lasting joy and also its stable causes, those of good action and enlightenment. The next logical wish is that beings may also be without pain and its negative origin. Two further wishes round off this inner disposition and make it complete: That others may have the greatest happiness that is totally beyond suffering and that they may feel the same strong love for all, making their actions limitless and ultimately meaningful.

Anger, on the other hand, halts one's natural disposition to help others and to wish them good things. It disturbs the human exchange, makes people lonely, and in addition destroys whatever good seeds for later happiness they have stored. Powerful forward looking motivation, on the other hand, unsentimental and without disturbing feelings, springs from one's unshakable belief in everyone's inherent buddha nature, in truth as all pervading like space, and in understanding that one is only able to imagine enlightenment outside of oneself because it already exists in oneself. On this basis of right view rests the consequential way of the accomplishers, the level of the Buddhist yogi.

Boundless Space and Joy — The Level of Accomplishing Yogis

When studying the most exciting of Buddha's teachings, his Diamond Way methods, a short summary is useful to clarify the steps and general principles which make one's practice on this ultimate level fruitful. While aware of the laws of karma and motivated by the wish to benefit others and the above mentioned wisdoms, here awareness expresses its absolute aspects by awakening the full potential of body and speech. Enabling mind to first taste and then trust its own perfection, faster than any other method, these two steps to realization may work in tandem.

Mentioned frequently in Buddhism as essential, positive actions free up space for insights to arise. When enough hindrances have been removed, that which is between, behind, and which knows the passing feelings and thoughts, emerges. Being now aware of itself, mind is king. As mind is always the radiant conscious space pervading all times and directions, enlightenment is everybody's true nature. Therefore, no truth may possibly be added to it, and the teaching of any Buddha will surely remove the veils which keep mind from recognizing itself. While the sun of accumulated good impressions climbs and the fog of ignorance evaporates, a practitioner's happiness and intuitive insight grows. This again proves further good actions to be the way to go.

As it becomes evident how little distance most beings have from their feelings and how controlled they are by them, the wish arises to protect them, but in an empowering way. If one acts out of pity and deals mainly with their weaknesses and immediate needs, one creates dependence and actually harms them. The right feeling here is tough compassion, helping them to find their own strong qualities and reach values that are meaningful in the long run.

As good impressions and wisdom grow, meaningless behavior is automatically discarded. In the end everything fits. Wherever one looks, every experience is pure. There is only happiness inside and fulfillment outside. From this position, mind gladly lets go of constricting habits, ever more frequently enjoying its indwelling radiant energy, its timeless clear light.

Because this beyond personal state is something ultimate, the ego feels its dominance come under attack. It then defends itself with thoughts like, "My clear light lasted longer than his last week," or, "Now I will soon be enlightened." The feeling of loss that such moments produce makes many believe that they have fallen back, but in reality such thoughts mean nothing. The sun of enlightening awareness always shines; one just experienced some passing clouds. If one ignores them, even the strongest habits will gradually lose their energy and expose their artificial nature. Untouched by concepts, mind will then rest ever longer in its blissful presence.

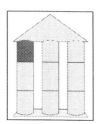

Knowledge and View:
Buddha — The Mirror of One's Own Mind

Seeing outer and inner events as mutually dependent, caught in a flow of constant change and not truly existing, as is indeed their essence, expresses mind's wisdom aspect. If at the same time one has consciously built up vast quantities of those good impressions, frequently called merit, a jump of courage will take one to the yogi level. This is of immense importance due to the skillfulness of the methods used.

On the Small Way liberation is the ultimate goal. According to the texts, unsurpassable enlightenment on the Great Way takes three countless *kalpas* (eons). Yet the lives of colorful yogis like Marpa, Milarepa, Rechungpa, Gampopa and today the Karmapas and Shamarpas, to speak of only one Tibetan lineage, show how Diamond Way practices and deep confidence may bring even difficult people to enlightenment in just one lifetime. On this level, also due to impressions from former lives, knowing becomes spontaneous insight beyond concepts.

Here, Buddha is no longer a historical teacher or an energy that is separate from oneself, but rather a mirror to one's potential. He expresses an infinitely attractive reality, which one wishes to absorb and never lose. While disturbing feelings, veils of confusion, and clumsy habits gradually disappear, states of grateful bliss grow longer and more frequent. Arriving on this third and ultimate level, and protected by unbroken bonds to one's teacher, quick progress is assured. Proceeding from the insight that experiencer, the object experienced, and the experience itself are interdependent, mutually conditioning, and aspects of the same totality, reaching the goal is only a matter of time.

FOUR BUDDHA STATES

The Diamond Way and the Great Way both describe buddha nature and the richness of space through four buddha states. They show that every appearance is mind. The aim of Buddha's teachings is to constantly experience timeless intuitive insight. This is called the Truth State (Sanskrit: *Dharmakaya*, Tibetan: *Cheuku*). It is inseparable from space, manifests through its own power, and is all pervading. When mind realizes its indestructible quality, that its essence is no object or thing, it becomes deeply fearless. This quality is the unshakable basis for attaining all perfections.

Mind's clarity, meaning its talents and gift of perception, springs from the Truth State. It is closer to life. Beings greatest joys arise when they are fully in the here and now and forget to expect anything. Then inner and outer richness playfully meet. This experience makes a giant wave of fulfillment and meaning well up within as mind experiences its freshness. Here the very power of awareness is most important while the objects and situations appearing are more secondary and one rejoices in mind's many sided possibilities. This experience is called the Joy State (Sanskrit: *Sambhogakaya*, Tibetan: *Longku*). It emerges from the Truth State for the good of all and is brought forth by one's own surplus.

When experiencing the wish for everyone to be happy, realizing that one is singular and the others are many, it becomes natural to want to help others. The compassionate Emanation State (Sanskrit: *Nirmanakaya*, Tibetan: *Tulku*) thus manifests this desire to benefit others. Many fine women and men who possess natural confidence in mind's and life's basic goodness and unselfishly help others belong in this noble class.

The first seven levels of energetic bodhisattva teachers, where one does not yet see the buddhas, may be called incarnations and the final three, to whom buddha forms appear, emanations. In the Joy State one has the choice to either go fully beyond and become everything that benefits beings or retain one's primary qualities that one's former students will readily recognize. Confidence will then appear and hopefully the lessons of that next round will be exciting and limitless.

In the Great Seal teachings, like those given by the Karmapas, which clearly point out mind's timeless essence, the Enlightened State (mind's full functioning) is often compared to water. Mind manifesting in its intuitive Truth State would be like humidity, not visible but able to penetrate everything, like all pervading information. Clouds that condense playfully and travel freely everywhere represent mind's rich Joy State. Mind's active love, in the Emanation State, would be the rain that nourishes plants and the snow or ice that protect animals from the cold. In their wholeness and despite their apparent differences, all are water, the Essential State (Sanskrit: *Svabhavikakaya*, Tibetan: *Ngowonygiku*). Mind expresses itself in these different meaningful ways, yet essentially remaining the same.

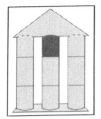

Meditation: Melting with Enlightenment

When Buddha's students had confidence in their inherent perfection, he taught the manifold methods of the Diamond Way. To this day these transmissions of view and meditation on the ultimate level have freed or enlightened countless students, letting them discover their minds to be radiant space and free of all limitations. Such practices remove all veils from mind and allow one to perceive the world as a pure land, enabling one to act like a buddha until one becomes one. Three essential qualities of mind: awareness, energy, and capacity for devoted fascination serve practitioners as handles for its recognition. Each enables states of heightened awareness in which meditators experience themselves as luminous, blissful, limitless, complete, and needing nothing from anywhere.

Combining view, meditation and action, such methods make the beyond personal experiences of practitioners grow; action and insights attained are confirmed in daily life. From the fearless knowledge that mind is indestructible, self arising joy appears and is expressed as kind and useful deeds in everybody. Such activities influence one's environment and awaken confidence in others, that they may accomplish the same.

When analyzing the meditations of Diamond Way Buddhism, what has often been presented as shrouded in mystery is really just applied common sense. Using all the levels and methods that Buddha gave, their effectiveness is awesome.

First in each meditation one focuses on one's breath, thereby quieting one's mind and preparing oneself with the four considerations of one's situation in life. Then one turns to the same four observations that today, two and a half millennia later, still effectively motivate every Great Way and Diamond Way meditation. They first point out the precious and rare possibility of having met with the teachings of a Buddha and to develop mightily in this lifetime. Next, they make evident the impermanence of all things and give convincing reasons to practice immediately. Thirdly, they remind one of cause and effect, making clear that all determine their future through their current thoughts, words, and actions. And finally, they give two excellent reasons for consciously using one's life: That having no other cause other than indestructible mind itself, one cannot do much for others if confused or in pain oneself and that the immense bliss of enlightenment is without end.

Then as a protection and inner direction for others and oneself, one takes refuge in the Three Jewels. First comes the goal (Buddha), mind's full development. Secondly his teachings (Dharma) that bring one there and thirdly in the bodhisattvas (Sangha), one's friends and helpers on the way. Then above all one takes refuge in the Three Roots of quick development: the blessing, inspiration, and protective ability of one's lama. This activates both the outer and inner powerfields and prepares one for deep work with one's store consciousness, for establishing the highest view, and activating enlightened energies. The motivation on the Diamond Way, as with the Great Way, is always to develop oneself in order to be unshakable and truly useful to others.

After taking Refuge, two doors to enlightenment stand open, the one of awareness and that of identification. If one also wants to do the exciting exercises activating the energies of body and mind, the 111,111 repetitions of the Four Foundational Practices, *Ngondro*, become necessary. They are character forming and I deeply advise taking the time.

One's inner bonds with the Refuge are strengthened through the first Foundational Practice, called Prostrations. These hard physical exercises straighten the energy flow through our body. They thereby remove countless harmful bodily impressions from this and former lifetimes before they mature and transform one's body from a difficult master into a useful servant. If done with the view of benefiting others, Prostrations truly express the Bodhisattva Promise.

The next practice, the meditation on the Buddha Diamond Mind, activated by his one hundred and his six syllable mantras, effectively cleans out and transforms unpleasant impressions and habits from one's speech and mind accumulated over limitless lifetimes. Giving away 111,111 perfect universes in the Mandala practice, the third Foundational Practice, plants powerful seeds of future richness and joy in one's life.

Finally during the last and extended meditation on the lama, one deepens gratitude for the lineage and its direct transmission, which one receives through one's own teacher. It is like ring meeting hook. The student's openness and the teacher's blessing make this meditation a direct step to the Great Seal, to experiencing the nature of one's mind. Since all Four Foundational Practices are tantric (total) involving body, speech and mind and are repeated so many times, they accompany most meditators for several years and have a noticeable effect.

During the 1,500 years Buddhism existed in India, the great variety of advanced Diamond Way meditations were divided into three classes. Among them, one was secretly taught because its methods are dangerous to the unprepared. It is the **Way of Methods**, which works with deep breathing and the awakening of inner energies. The directly accessible **Way of Insight** works with awareness while the third and rarely mentioned but highly effective **Way of Identification** (Sanskrit: *Guru Yoga*, Tibetan: *Lami Naljor*) was formally transmitted only in small groups to the most devoted students.

As an expression of his trust in our power to keep our bonds and because of its extremely high value for the idealistic West, the 16th Karmapa wanted this third way to be the main practice in his Diamond Way centers. The meditations on one's lama, which build on the deep confidence between student and teacher, have been immensely effective among the lay Western Diamond Way Karma Kagyu students worldwide. The Way of Identification includes and freely uses the methods and views of the two other ways as well.

The richness of philosophical and psychological methods used in Tibetan Buddhism is unique in the world. It is also little known. Yet the guiding principles are easy. In all ways, Small and Great, it is always simply and essentially a matter of two steps: First orienting oneself towards and then accomplishing the perfect qualities displayed.

THE WAY OF INSIGHT

Whoever understands better through abstractions than through images will delight in Buddhas Way of Insight. The Tibetan hero Marpa received it in its full extent from his second main teacher Maitripa in Northern India 950 years ago. These methods are completely logical, all encompassing, and fully compatible with our lives today. However, a deep and practical realization, especially one that contains also a strong foundation of life experience and humor, is much more rare than one may think. The teachings require maturity, but also masses of good karma and the guidance of an experienced teacher. It is advisable to enter this way after completing the many repetitions of the Ngondro. The massive buildup of good impressions achieved, counteract the dangerous white wall effect of the soft, lazy, sleepy, peaceful state that can appear and so easily robs mind of its power to act.

Noble tigers may turn into sheep by attempting to do calming meditation or by simply quieting mind for too long, without receiving the necessary transmission and insight from an inspiring teacher. Without such empowerments, mental veils are not removed but simply ignored or covered up. Mind will then retract, losing its natural freshness and will not realize its radiant essence of intuitive bliss. Confused solitary meditators and docile unclear groups worldwide serve as warnings of this danger.

On the Way of Insight, mind first experiences its timeless wisdom in brief but highly conscious moments, recognizing first its desired objects and then the world as being dreamlike and illusory, empty of any lasting nature. Then as one's outer teacher, the lama, supplies the inner teacher, one's ability to discriminate with the right information, mind gradually extends its *a-ha* states, until their combination brings about the secret ultimate teacher, one's own matured awareness.

Focusing on an outer object and observing the breath at one's nostrils without evaluating thoughts are widely used tools for holding mind. Some of these practices are used by experience based non-Buddhist religions as well, though the goals sought by these traditions will vary, like bringing a balanced long life to the Taoist and willpower, Shakti, to the Hindu. On the three Buddhist ways, the steps of calming and holding mind and the arising of insight into its nature are found everywhere.

On the ultimate level of the Diamond Way, the full potential of body, speech, and mind is quickly accomplished through identifying with the lama. Seeing him or her as a buddha while following the formless approach of the Great Seal teachings, one will directly recognize mind as luminous space. The periods of meditation and the times in between will thus gradually develop the same taste; then body, speech, and mind will effortlessly fuse with any situation. Following this way, one may relax in the pure land of unlimited possibilities and effortlessly put these qualities into action, benefiting ever more beings.

All of Buddha's meditations obtain this goal with more or less effective methods, pressing varying amounts of enlightening buttons in the practitioner and deepening levels of understanding their ultimately empty nature appear. For those who can use the Diamond Way, its two direct steps towards obtaining their buddha nature consist of the developing phase *Che Rim* (Tibetan), the invocation of the buddhas meditated upon, including their mantras, and the completion phase the *Dzog Rim* (Tibetan) where one melts together with them and dissolves into conscious space. Conclusively one reappears with their qualities and views into a pure land and surrounded by potential buddhas. Sounds here are mantras and all thoughts wisdom, simply because they show mind's potential.

Depending on one's tendencies toward desire, anger, or confusion there are major differences in the approach and skillfulness even when using these highest practices. Since life is short, each person should therefore choose, with the help of their teacher, which group of meditations best fits one's nature. Here the key practices are Mother Tantra for those with predominant desire, Father Tantra for the angry/proud types, and Non-Dual Tantra for those suffering from confusion.

Meditations on one's teacher, Guru Yoga or Lami Naljor, provide the broadest and the most total transformation into the pure view. In these mediations the anger type meditator will naturally extend the controlled building up phase, those with much desire will spend more time in the sweet phase of oneness, while the confusion type will hold on to whatever details the text provides.

In the West, the Mother Tantra seems to especially attract Kagyu practitioners; the Father Tantra, the Nyingma; and the Non-Dual Tantra, the Gelugpa. To the best of my understanding, the Sakyapa preserve and write important commentaries on all of the tantras.

THE WAY OF METHODS

Since 1050 AD, Tibetans wanting to explore the enlightening energies dwelling in the body-mind totality sought out the teachings in the Way of Methods. They are exceedingly profound and were especially received on Marpa's second stay with his main teacher Naropa. Even today a physically strong yogi, who has completed preliminaries and meditations on the lady energy Buddha Red Wisdom (Sanskrit: *Vajrayogini*, Tibetan: *Dorje Phagmo*), may reach into a truly abundant toolbox. The Way of Methods today primarily attracts people who have the conditions for meditating in retreats for long periods of time or have obtained strong results from such practices in former lives. The yogi Milarepa, Marpa's student, is a timeless example, meditating nearly naked for thirty years in the high central Himalayas. Hidden groups of such people still exist in Tibet today. Opening all wheels and energy lines in his body, Milarepa's inspiring songs are now available in bookshops of Western countries.

For his students to transcend their everyday habits of

perception, 2,450 years ago Buddha manifested the countless peaceful and protective, female and male, single and united forms that correspond to the potential enlightened qualities of beings. Buddha emanated out single energy forms when sharing the first three Buddhist tantric levels: known as *Kriya*, *Charya*, and *Yoga*. Through these he reached people who did not yet have full confidence in the basic purity of all appearances, especially in sexuality.

His initiations into the fourth Buddhist tantric level, the unsurpassable *Maha-Anuttara* yogas, inspire those who due to massive good karma, have full confidence in their buddha nature. Here Buddha transformed his own body into standing or sitting, male and female buddha forms in union. These always appear as holograms, radiating limitless energy, facing each other for the circulation and balancing of the female space and the male bliss in their bodies. Receiving their empowerment from a holder of the transmission is all important and the blessing fields they condense, along with their colors, positions, features, peaceful or protective attributes, syllables, and mantras awaken the enlightened qualities of their practitioners.

While the ultimate experience of mind is always radiant aware space, its truth essence on the level of blissful play and its activity is expressed through the buddha forms of all four types mentioned earlier. They manifest as pacifying, enriching, fascinating, and powerfully protecting. Only the united aspects, however, transmit the fullness of enlightenment. Male or female forms that appear alone express only half. For someone who has the necessary maturity and can hold the bliss state between meditations, the practices involving the buddhas or one's lama in union make it possible to reach enlightenment in a single lifetime. This can be seen in the many life stories of yogis, so far mainly from central East Asia.

The peace giving and single buddhas can be invoked for their general blessing; but whoever wants to meditate on united or protective buddha forms should first receive an empowerment, called *Wang* in Tibetan. One also needs a permission, a *Lung*, for all such practices. This transmission is given by hearing the text read aloud in Tibetan by a recognized teacher. The instructions on how to use the texts are called *Tri* and are another precondition for success. One receives these orally from somebody with experience, who knows the practice and has done it. Among yogis and outside the monasteries, things are less complicated, using methods of transmission known as *Gomlung*. Today's guided Diamond Way meditations, in one's own language and led by somebody holding their bonds of friendship and trust, are highly useful examples of this direct method.

If a teacher keeps his style and avoids weaknesses that would erode his motivated students' confidence, the enlightened seeds planted in their store consciousnesses by a Gomlung or a combination of Wang, Lung, and Tri transmissions will stay and grow. They are the students' living access to the powerfields of their lamas and the buddha forms invoked by their lineages. One may however begin the Foundational Practices, Ngondro, which are a part of the Way of Methods, and meditate on the peaceful and single buddhas while anticipating the transmission.

After a time of meditation, depending on the imprints brought along from former lives, a lack of expectations lets joyful moments break through. Then ever more often students trust themselves to be buddha forms of light and energy, surrounded by pure lands. Sounds are then mantras and all thoughts, even the most ridiculous are wisdom, simply because they show mind's potential. States of bliss can then be produced or prolonged through conscious deep breathing, while the blessing of one's lineage opens the energy channels in one's body.

With the view of the Great Seal that space and joy are inseparable, any of the six energy practices of Naropa, including the meditation for conscious dying, Phowa, lead to quick realization. Guided meditations in one's own language are immediately understandable and make today's transmission of these teachings easy. Still only a rare few, even among Tibetans, grasp the full meaning and structure of the formal empowerments, which have remained unchanged since Buddha's time. They have the structure of invocations, which are stopped at important points to transmit the accumulated blessing.

For the better enjoyment of what will hopefully remain a strong source of inspiration and an open door to enlightened mind's most attractive aspects, here is a short explanation of what the rituals during an empowerment mean. each ceremony begins with the symbolic cleansing of body, speech, and mind of all those present. That takes place either at the entrance to the hall by rinsing out one's mouth or later by the lama pouring saffron water over a convex metal hand mirror that reflects all in the room. During this process the purifying 100-syllable Diamond Mind mantra is repeated. Then the lama purifies the environment, attracting all disturbing energies by offering a cake that is then carried from the room. After that a protective field is created and surrounds the place. The teacher then reads the history of the text in Tibetan, mentioning when and from which line of teachers he received these transmissions. At this point everyone repeats the Refuge in short clusters of syllables and generates the bodhisattva attitude by stating their intention to use any development that develops from the initiation for the good of all.

After this the actual empowerment happens, which awakens mind's ability to recognize itself through meditating on a particular buddha form. There are two models for this part of the ceremony that are commonly used. In the simpler style of empowerment, which requires no promises, the blessing of body, speech, mind, qualities, and activity of the chosen buddha form is activated and transmitted. This is called *Jenang* in Tibetan, meaning permission. During the other more extensive kind of empowerment that belongs to the Anuttara-Tantra and which may entail promises of later practice (always check first!), one receives the so-called Vase empowerment, the Secret empowerment, the Wisdom Awareness empowerment, and the Word empowerment through symbolic objects and concentration on colored lights. In both cases the teacher may give an additional blessing through a Torma empowerment, which binds everything together.

During the Vase empowerment, the lama or his representatives touch students' heads with a symbolic vase meditated to contain a specific buddha and also share a blessed liquid from it to drink, a buddha's essence. This purifies the body and grants the power to experience one's own body as the buddha's light form. The Secret empowerment in which one receives nectar from the united buddhas opens the middle energy channel, the five central energy wheels around them, and their 72,000 spokes throughout the body. It purifies speech and transmits the power to use the buddha's mantra and meditate on the inner energies. The Wisdom Awareness empowerment transmits the blessing of space and bliss inseparable. It purifies one's mind and gives the blessing to meditate on yogic union. Here the buddha's distinguishing attributes, ornaments, and partners flow to the meditator and are absorbed in one's heart. Finally the Word empowerment lets one share the lama's awareness space. Either by showing a symbolic gesture or object, like a crystal, or by reciting some words about the nature of mind, the lama directly imparts instructions on the nature of mind to students. Doing or saying something totally unexpected, he creates a shared space beyond concepts. This experience cuts through to the ultimate state of the Great Seal. Thus body, speech, and mind together are purified. A seed is sown that enables one to partake in the timeless unity and essence of all phenomena.

From the energy fields of the buddhas invoked and the psychologically profound process of empowerments, both coarse disturbances as well as many subtle veils in the recipients' body, speech, and minds are removed. In addition, the feedback from the representations used, the powerfields established, and vibrations of mantras and seed syllables activated, countless liberating seeds are planted in the store consciousness of everyone present and develop every inherent possibility to experience mind. Most important in empowerments of all kinds is their ability to bring about a connection between one's own beyond personal and spontaneously emerging awareness and the information of timeless space. In this way they lead to this full realization, one's only real refuge. When students take this highest view from one life to the next, they will again make contact with buddhas on the Diamond Way level and grow without end. Whatever happens or does not happen will then be ever more recognized as mind's richness and free play.

Whoever can maintain this ultimate view shines. It forms the strongest protection in life and brings lasting bliss. The motivation level of compassion and wisdom is likewise strengthened through this highest view. It produces skill and intuition and trickles down to the domain of cause and effect, making one kind. If all beings are buddhas in pure lands, harmful deeds become meaningless.

If such effective methods are transmitted through a trustworthy lama, representing an unbroken lineage, they strengthen the inner development of students. They awaken powerfields that follow them from life to life, remain active, and transform outer events into teachers. The very first syllable of a mantra or the first thought of a trusted lama or buddha form condenses their protective power in space and the phases of dissolving with them used in Diamond Way meditations lead one to a gradual absorption of their beyond personal qualities.

Though they can only partially change karma, empowerments, guided meditations, pointing out instructions, and blessings thus all bring about a connection to timeless, unlimited insight. While expanding and strengthening this bond, one is already living in a pure land. One already experiences the present situation as essentially perfect and sees all beings and things without colored glasses of disturbing emotions, expectations, and habits.

THE WAY OF IDENTIFICATION —
ACCOMPLISHING THE TEACHER'S QUALITIES AND POWERFIELD

Resting in the states of bliss and space inseparable, engendered by the meditations on buddha forms and their mantras, produces the finest of spiritual qualities. Experience shows that experiencing the ordinary on the highest level happens when a teacher's ability to inspire and a student's idealistic openness meet. Their union vastly increases the effectiveness of any meditation. Known as Guru Yoga or Lami Naljor, this method was singled out by the 16th Gyalwa Karmapa and given to my wife Hannah and myself as the main practice for our worldwide Diamond Way centers. Easy to approach and enabling people to recognize and learn from meaningful qualities in all of life's situations, it is an exceedingly skillful tool for developing identification and trust.

Partaking in the view of a realized lama, one gains certainty that potential enlightenment is already present in everyone and can be realized. This exchange is so all encompassing and impressive that one enters a mental state of bliss and deep meaning, a so-called Pure Land. One can no longer forget it, and appearing for ever longer periods when one's practice is without expectation, such a view will enrich every aspect of one's way. The main object to accomplish after a Kagyu transmission is to increasingly experience that which looks through our eyes and hears through our ears and remain aware both during meditation and in daily life. For that mighty task, a teacher is indispensable and as the great lama Lopon Tsechu Rinpoche often said, "Above all one must keep the connection to the teacher who first showed one the nature of mind. Otherwise deep dissatisfaction appears and one's development simply stalls."

From 1050 to 1950 AD, when the communist Chinese first attacked Eastern Tibet, these methods, providing direct access to mind, were passed on in Tibet in their fullness. Without interruption and as a living stream, both view and methods were transmitted from teachers to students, who then became teachers. In Europe and gradually all over the West, this transmission has continued since 1972. Therefore, in Diamond Way centers worldwide, whoever teaches represents the Karma Kagyu lineage: the 16th Karmapa, Rangjung Rigpe Dorje, who established the practices; his 17th incarnation, the Karmapa Trinley Thaye Dorje; and the root lama representing the lineage, the one students know and ultimately trust.

All who have confidence in mind's limitless potential recognize their abilities in the mirror held by a skillful teacher. Already at one's first taking of refuge, a connection is activated between the inherent insight of the students' minds and the timeless wisdom of all buddhas. Every event can now be used for growth. Pleasant situations appear as blessings to be shared with others, while difficult experiences liberate one's store consciousness from countless causes of later suffering. It is joyful and makes sense to use one's experiences for the good of others and to share all blessings with them.

Buddhism shows how things are and only aims to bring people to maturity. This frees Buddhist teachers from any dishonest roles of installing beliefs or having to sell others illogical messages. Instead they are supposed to know and embody what they teach. Their job is to make students independent and capable by reflecting back their inherent, fearless, and joyful compassion. This is a hand-me-down process, open to the methods of modern communication and may therefore benefit countless open minds. As each generation of students become teachers and come to trust their own ability to help others, their students will develop beyond personal qualities and express them, inspiring again the next wave. Therefore the meditation of becoming inseparable from the teacher is the fastest and most useful way for those fortunate ones who can use it. Behaving like one's teacher or the Buddha until one has acquired such qualities, lets timeless and limitless qualities grow in anyone's mind.

Throughout history and up to the present, transmission lineages consist of students who realize mind's nature with the methods and views of their schools within the blessing stream of their teacher's awareness. This happens today, when after sufficient practice, students become knowledgeable teachers or lamas themselves and pass on this living stream. A historical example of a teacher's importance goes back to the year 1050 AD in Tibet. At that time the hero Marpa, father of the lay Diamond Way Karma Kagyu transmission, brought Buddhism over the Himalayas to Tibet, for the second time, after its destruction under the shamanist King Langdharma in 800 AD. He trained and taught his main student Milarepa, who then had two main students: Rechungpa, the independent minded yogi with a keen sense of the goodness of women, carried on the lay transmission while Gampopa, the first monk in the lineage, created its central monastic branch.

One day in Northern India when Marpa was studying with Naropa, his main teacher, and deep in meditation, the Buddha Oh Diamond (Sanskrit: *Hevajra*, Tibetan: *Kye Dorje),* suddenly condensed at Marpa's side. Big as a house, blue, transparent, and radiating like a thousand suns, Hevajra's many hands held skull cups and he embraced his blue consort, Not-I (Sanskrit: *Nairamya*, Tibetan: *Dagmema)*, in standing union. Marpa was deeply moved and Naropa, who probably looked like any other old Indian, wrinkled and burned black from the sun, asked him, "Now you see him and me. Which one will you greet first?" Marpa's thinking is not hard to follow. He bowed to the buddha form. But Naropa laughed. "Wrong choice!" he said, "With us everything is the teacher." Then Naropa dissolved the huge powerfield of Hevajra into rainbow light and drew it into his heart.

In the West and today the teacher retains such vital importance to Buddha's Diamond Way. His blessing shows the world to be a dream that can be mastered. His or her spontaneous and effortless activity convinces one of basic unity. One recognizes that the experiencer, the object experienced, and the act of experiencing must all be interdependent, inseparable, and parts of the same totality. As with the other means used in meditation, the formless methods of experiencing mind's space insight and the complete tool of identification with and dissolving with buddha forms, a natural state of knowing they are aspects of one's trusted lama arises and one realizes the Great Seal of ultimate meaning. Then it becomes less important which of the ways one uses to get to this under-standing. Its highest view contains everything and is unique. It has an unshakeable foundation: the inherent buddha nature of all beings, a true way to experience a meaningful life using the finest of methods for absorption and human growth, and above all, the ultimate goal of full enlightenment. Every concept pales in comparison with such total awareness.

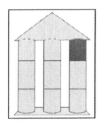

Action: Practice Being Like a Buddha

The Diamond Way view and the entire structure just described are based on the deep insight that the pure realms of awareness are more true than any ordinary experience. Because highest truth is highest joy, one decides never to leave that state. In Buddha's teachings this does not mean positive thinking, the strenuous attempt to avoid noticing suffering. What brings liberating meaning to any expression of mind's potential is the realization that everything is ultimately the free play of space. The subject here is the timeless radiance of mind's mirror, undisturbed by its conditioned and changing images. On this level one knows in the marrow of one's bones that highest truth is highest joy. One experiences mind as fearless and playful, shining, rich, and powerful in and of itself. Thus one always remains and acts in the moment, is aware and compassionate. As the experiencer looking through one's eyes increasingly perceives its essence as non-substantive radiating light, every tightness or fear gradually disappears. The growing knowledge that one's true essence is timeless and cannot be destroyed brings ultimate certainty. From then on one is at home everywhere regardless of what happens.

The transforming insight that brings about this realization should be made of a daily occurrence: that one is neither the body that will get old, sick, and certainly die nor the flow of changing thoughts. What looks through beings' eyes and listens through their ears, here and now, is conscious and unlimited space. It is totally beyond coming and going, birth and death.

As fearlessness is accordingly accomplished, everything appears ever more fresh and new, exciting just because it can or may happen. Both birth and death then show mind's playful variety. At that point, hope and fear fade, and one is instead fascinated by the richness of what is conscious. From then on it is less important what films are playing. It is more essential then that the screen has no holes and that the projector works! When mind's awareness is no longer obstructed by evaluating its images, all events, outer as well as inner, appear as fresh and exciting simply because they are possible.

Up to this point, a practitioner may enjoy the protective distance of thinking, "Yesterday I was jealous, then I became angry, and just now I am confused. How exciting! Let's see what tomorrow will bring!" From here the experience of radiant space increasingly takes over. The mirror becomes visible behind its images. One perceives the ocean underneath its waves and this provides the opportunities to act meaningfully and steadfastly accomplishes what is in front of one's nose. Whoever feels mind's essential power and richness will naturally express its unlimited potential. Thus one will perform whatever benefits all and secures human rights and freedoms into the most distant future.

Self absorbed wishes towards one's own pleasures are then only of passing interest. Instead mind's natural surplus makes every experience increasingly broad and deep, and it becomes evident that everyone can develop boundlessly. With such promising potential, many gladly commit to the welfare of more and more beings, helping them discover their abilities, and enabling them to be free! One now has real power and relies on one's own long range views, rather than following the changing and stop-gap opinions of others. Whoever can keep aware of beings' potential for transformation, while at the same time experiencing outer and inner worlds on the level of purity, will make few mistakes.

Decisive for any development are the skills and methods used. One may get to enlightenment by digging with one's hands, or a shovel, or a backhoe, or by walking, driving, or flying. Because life is short and habits strong, it is essential to use the most effective of means on the levels relevant to people.

For those attracted to the Small Way of Southern Buddhism, as mentioned above, the main wish above all is to avoid the causes of one's own suffering. This way is long and requires ongoing and repeated evaluations of one's own karma. One is here continually occupied with actions, words, and thoughts, focusing on patterns of reactive behavior. On the Great Way of Methods, wisdom and compassion are one's guides. If one can keep such inner states well balanced mind's development will be broad. Here one needs to pay heed to one's own mental freshness and notice how one behaves among friends. If fixed concepts dominate, lack of human exchange will make one lonely and mainly relating to oneself will make life joyless.

Success on the third and ultimate level, the Way of Identification, elucidated in this chapter, stands or falls with one's view. Here one must always be conscious of how one experiences the world. Are feelings of growth, purity, and freshness involved in every event? Does one generally see a potential buddha in others and in oneself? If one answers "Yes!" spontaneous richness and meaning are already growing and everything good will manifest effortlessly. Ever more convincingly, perfection will then express itself as the timeless essence of all things.

Changes in awareness take root over many lives and are directed through one's practice. Working with the methods and attitude of the Small Way puts only a few chips on the roulette table and is labor intensive. As the sutras state, with the given methods recognizing the unreality of the *I* and experiencing liberation, arhatship that is connected to that realization takes innumerable world cycles. If one only aims for an end to one's own difficulties, one also remains vulnerable during the process. This is because one lacks teachings on the second stage of emptiness, where one realizes the ego and the world to be without any lasting reality. With this view one also misses the intention to protect the countless beings with whom one would otherwise be in solidarity.

The noble attitude which combines all beings' search for happiness with the additional beyond personal insight into the empty and dream like nature of the outer world, explains the flexibility and effectiveness of northern Great Way Buddhism. Although it can still take three countless kalpas to reach enlightenment, it is much more satisfactory.

Only Diamond Way methods use all possibilities of body, speech, and mind, activating a meditator's sexuality, imagination, disturbing feelings, and power of identification. They are truly fast, historically bringing several Kagyu hard cases like Marpa and Milarepa to the goal in one life. Transforming the energy, courage, and daydreams of beings such states are powerful agents on their way to enlightenment. One can now let a thief come to an empty house. When the connections to one's lama work, there exists no more complete means. Ultimate wisdom now directs beings' inherent qualities towards the absolute goal.

Proceeding from the crane of highest confidence is the Diamond Way. One first pours the foundation of fearless right action, then places the walls, and finally raises the beautiful roof. With that, the house stands. With the above understanding, the level of an accomplishing yogi is already an application of the Great Seal.

The Highest View – The Great Seal

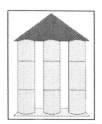

Being Buddha's ultimate teaching and the level of reference for this book, here is a final look at the levels of growth and enlightenment obtained on one's approach to the Great Seal. The full information for the basis of the way to and goal of enlightenment was established both in India and Tibet and may be gleaned from twenty five verses given 700 years ago by the great third Karmapa Rangjung Dorje.[4] This expression of the Great Seal (Sanskrit: *Mahamudra*, Tibetan: *Chagchen*) is unique. It uses all tools of insight to introduce students to mind's timeless nature. The accomplishment of these methods means a life fully in the here and now, unfettered by duality.

Like all healthy growth, these teachings build on good karma. All who free their store consciousness of its major disturbing influences and instead charge it with sufficient good impressions will automatically develop a strong confidence in the basic goodness of things. This trust allows for mind's awareness to emerge ever more frequently between and around its experiences. Mind will then recognize itself as the limitless conscious space from which these experiences appear, that which knows them, where they play, and to which they return. From here the continuation to a direct and non-conceptual perception of mind is close and the traveler, way and goal then become a blissful unfolding of all qualities of body, speech, and mind. The Great Seal is the highest view of the Kagyu Diamond Way and encompasses the absolute level of empowerments in the other Buddhist schools of Tibet.

Although the ultimate teachings all point to aware space, beings are different and should be inspired according to their qualities and concepts. Therefore Buddha gave various methods for each human type, supplying for the highest levels of awareness 21,000 different means to access mind, called the Buddhist tantras. These include the Great Seal as the view guiding energy work, deep breathing, and other methods. Our sister lineage, the Nyingmas, often see their highest view, Dzogchen, as unrelated to any other practice.

The general emotional tone of the Kagyu lineage is one of devotion and gratitude and its Diamond Way centers therefore mainly attract people who are desire oriented. Feeling drawn to the Lotus Buddha family transforms attachment and the long and playful completion phases of mixing with the lamas and buddhas in Mother Tantras recognize mind through direct experience. Desire people thereby enjoy life's effortless play of possibilities as the fresh, new, and self arisen richness of every moment. If mind is symbolized by water, they know this substance by swimming in it. The boundless experience on this highest level brings about an unfiltered awareness in every life situation: one acts more and more from the potential of what is. For that reason only mind's limitless and perceiving space is recognized as being real. The maturity that arises from this joyful experience is most attractive. Whoever understands that it is more important not to get distracted by thoughts, than to judge them, will work without wear and tear. The depth of the ocean is more meaningful than any waves and the mirror is more brilliant than its ever-changing images. This view releases immediate power in everyone, allowing people to work together well in groups and all are rich!

Whenever anger and pride dominate, mind's self-liberating quality manifests as the recognition that whatever manifests, will return to space again and disappear. This view is central to the Nyingmas, the old school of Tibet, and is called the Great Perfection (Sanskrit: *Maha Ati*, Tibetan: *Dzogchen*). Wanting to know exactly where they are and what exists, people of this type are attracted to the long and detailed building-up phases of the Father Tantra meditations.

The realization of emptiness and insubstantiality of all things thus reaches Westerners in different ways, depending on the methods. Whether one uses the intellect in debate or the whole mind in meditation, people should use their growing maturity and depth at all times and every situation. The speed of one's transformation and the development of maturity differ among people.

People in whom confusion is predominant or who like institutions and monastic lifestyles often prefer the teachings of the Great Middle Way. The analytic comprehension of emptiness is Rangtong, translated as empty in essence and meaning, that nothing has any existing personal nature. The Kagyu and Nyingma lineages just mentioned, as well as the less pretentious way of the Red Hat Sakya school, called Lamdre in Tibetan (literally meaning way and fruit), touch all aspects of being through their transforming power. On the levels of insight, as well as feelings and energy, these three schools employ total and non-conceptual methods for enlightening body, speech and mind. Their general understanding of emptiness is Shengtong.

The Sutra view translated as "empty of other" has brought accusations from the analytic Rangtong side, that its proponents are materialists and claim mind to be a "something" or "a clear light" which the Rangtong view denies. But the "other" which manifests – primarily the consciousness being aware of all phenomena – is also empty in nature. As the Shentong view conforms with life experience, however, it attracts a more hands-on and practical kind of people.

Finally, experienced yogis (accomplishers) who go beyond analysis and thought to the complete experience of body, speech and mind use the tantric term Detong. "De" here comes from the Tibetan word "Dewa", meaning bliss and it describes a profound meditation experience as mentioned for example in the Kalachakra Tantra. It denotes that the state of full realization is inseparable from highest bliss. This is expressed and meditated upon through the united female & male buddha forms which dissolves completely the perception of a separated outer and inner world of phenomena. Non-meditators only experience this state in flashes, like in love-making, motorcycling or skydiving. My own great Kagyu lamas used the term Detong often. It was their total certainty that there can be no enlightenment without highest, constant bliss - a truth so perfectly exemplified by the 16th Karmapa.

For seekers of spiritual excitement and totality, the Great Middle Way, by its very nature is less thrilling than the Great Seal and Great Perfection, the ways of direct experience. Still one can see that the representatives of Buddhist schools praise any ultimate insight which benefits beings. The third Karmapa confirmed this understanding in verse nineteen of his twenty five Great Seal wishes, "Mastering any of these ways leads to a realization of them all."

THE FOUR LEVELS OF THE GREAT SEAL
The way of the Great Seal begins by building up massive good

impressions in one's store consciousness and developing a growing confidence in one's teacher, who works tirelessly for others and must embody the goal. This is the foundation for all growth. When the student has stored enough joyful impressions, he or she will no longer seek their fulfillment outside of mind, which contains and is conscious of all situations. Instead he will move through the four levels of the Great Seal, each containing three steps.

The first level is the Yoga of One Pointedness and corresponds to the power of calming and holding mind (Tibetan: *Shiney*) until it becomes deep insight (Tibetan: *Lhaktong*). In the terminology of the Great Way, it corresponds to the first two of five levels on the path to enlightenment, that of accumulation and of union. Both come before one reaches the first Bodhisattva Level.

As mentioned above, the way of the Great Seal is based upon a concentrated build-up of one's best possible motivation. As one's mental state colors one's perception of the world, it awakens a growing confidence in the teacher who embodies the state for which one is striving. Such a surplus of good feeling and trust remains the basis of quick growth. When students have stored enough timeless sources of happiness inside, they may enjoy but will no longer depend on passing pleasures. The surplus of pleasant projections makes one rich and natural. The increasing perception that what happens in the here and now becomes naturally radiant and vastly more exciting and meaningful than anything artificial makes everything inauthentic fade and disappear.

The second level is The Yoga of Simplicity. Here one is uncontrived, plays no games, and simply enjoys the natural and constant play of phenomena. It corresponds to Lhaktong and encompasses the first through the eighth Bodhisattva Levels.

However, such simplicity is in no way superficial. It encompasses people's outer, inner, and secret levels. Even today, where old-fashioned inhibitions like shame of one's body or sexuality are becoming rare in healthy cultures, many are not really spontaneous. They still have difficulty setting their minds and speech equally free.

On this second non-artificial and uncontrived step of the Great Seal, one becomes both wide awake and free of inner blockages. Mind expresses perfected and unshakable awareness.

The third step, The Yoga of One Taste, appears when the meditator has bridged the separation between meditations and the periods between them, holding the pure view constantly. This is equivalent to the last three Bodhisattva Levels.

This third stage of One Taste is a major leap in one's development. Here the light of awareness pervades all experience with such clarity and strength that it can no longer be lost. From here on, the mirror is more important than the images it reflects and the depth of the ocean will not be forgotten when observing its changing waves. Even non-meditators may enjoy brief experiences of this state in their daily lives. They appear during the finest moments of making love, the slanting of the motorcycle in fast curves, the free fall before one opens one's parachute, but most of all as a result of perfect meditation. Here everything has the unique taste of simply happening. When this state is attained by consciously applying mind's view and power, it becomes reliable and mind's ability to experience penetrates every event, enlightenment is not far away.

The fourth state, The Yoga of Non-Meditation, is the ultimate aim. It is the perfect state of buddhahood. The name for this fourth stage is humorous, but what else can one express or be when all things are effortlessly accomplished and mind's bliss is endless? The enlightened awareness of space is then constant and one fully brings forth the potential of all beings. Every deed, word, and thought then expresses relative as well as absolute truth and brings lasting benefit. Giving and taking freely in the stream of the moment, one joyfully rides the tiger of spontaneous insight.

May all beings be and stay free.
Yours, Lama Ole

MEDITATIONS

Everyone knows states of meditation. The moments in life when something has been unexpectedly given to us, when joy spontaneously arose and everything was simply meaningful. The waves in mind's ocean became unimportant and one saw clearly, the dust fell off one's inner mirror and one understood. These are meditation experiences.

What brings lasting fulfilment without needing to add anything is one's mind, the awareness of the moment. This state is perfect and a right view combined with such meditation will make it last.

The following four meditations can help make any insight, like the ones found in this book, move from head to heart and enrich one's inner life. They can be practiced by any healthy mind without the guidance of a group or teacher. In addition to these mediations, whoever wants to invoke the highly effective buddha forms mentioned may also learn those practices in one of our 500 Diamond Way Buddhist centers and groups around the world.

It is helpful for any meditation to choose a quiet room and to sit either on a chair or in half or full lotus position. While following a text, one's back should be straight without being stiff, with the hands lying in the lap or on the knees. When thoughts appear, one simply pays no attention to them and they will disappear again.

Each of the following meditations corresponds to the different levels of Buddha's teachings. Though they are easy to understand and can be used by everyone, they contain and stabilize their essence. The first meditation is for people who wish to employ useful means while clarifying their stance towards Buddhism. The second and third represent methods used in the Small and Great Ways. They strengthen the inherent qualities of a practitioner.

The 16th Karmapa meditation shows the methods of the Diamond Way. When one realizes that the completion phase of the meditation does not unite something external or physical, but that awareness outside and inside' meet, one may rest effortlessly in mind's space and bliss and bring the gained surplus and love into the world.

Meditations can be ordered from:
www.diamondway.org/dharmashop
dharmashop@diamondway.org

RAINBOW LIGHT MEDITATION

We sit relaxed and straight, our right hand resting in our left palm and our thumbs touching lightly. If not seated in a chair our right calf rests on or in front of the left one and we draw our chin in slightly.

First, we calm the mind. We feel the formless stream of air coming and going at the tips of our noses and let thoughts and noises pass without evaluation.

Then we decide that we want to meditate to experience mind's richness and gain distance from any disturbing emotions. Not until then can one really help others.

At heart level, in the center of our chest, there now appears a tiny rainbow light. Gradually it expands through our body, totally filling it and dissolving all diseases and obstacles on its way. When we can stay with this awareness, our body shines like a lamp and light streams in all directions filling space. It dissolves the suffering of beings everywhere and the world now shines with great meaning and joy. All are in a pure land, full of limitless possibilities. Everything is self-liberating.

We emanate this light for as long as it feels natural.

Pause

When we end this meditation, the light returns and dissolves the outer world into open space. It shines into our bodies, which also dissolves and there is now only awareness with no form, center, or limit.

Pause

Then, like a fish jumping from the water, again a world appears. Everything vibrates with meaning. All beings are perfect in essence and our body and speech are tools for benefiting others.

Finally, we wish that the good that just appeared may become limitless and stream out to everyone. That it will remove their suffering and bring them the only lasting joy, the recognition of the nature of mind.

MEDITATION ON THE BREATH

(Meditation of the Small Way)

We sit as straight as we can without being tense. Then we focus on our body and try to completely relax our back, stomach, shoulders, hands, arms, neck, and head. We also relaxed our face. Our eyes and mouth are lightly closed.

We focus on the stream of air that comes and goes at the tip of our nose and breathe deeply a few of times. Then our attention turns to our breath, in the nose or the stomach. We breathe naturally and count repeatedly from 1 to 21 or think *in* and *out*, simply observing the breath and counting along with it. When a distraction appears in the mind or our thoughts wander off, we notice it and turn our focus back to our breath. If we like, we can say *thought* or *wandered off* with our inner voice.

Observe the breath.

Our thoughts come and go. They play in the past and in the future. We just notice this and return our attention to our breath. As we breathe in and out our stomach fills and empties with air.

Continue to observe the breath.

Our mind knows the state of being distracted. Whenever this happens, we return to our breath: inhale and exhale.

Continue to observe the breath.

When we want to finish the meditation, we open our eyes and become aware of the world around us again.

MEDITATION OF GIVING AND TAKING

(Meditation of the Great Way)

We feel the formless stream of air that comes and goes at the tip of our nose and let thoughts, feelings, and sounds pass by without evaluating them.

When mind becomes calm, we take refuge in the Buddha as our goal, his Teachings as our way, and in the Bodhisattvas, our friends and companions on the way. We now want to meditate so we become able to benefit all beings and understand the non-reality of all conditioned existence.

We experience the pain of all beings as a black cloud that surrounds them and we fearlessly inhale it. Once the cloud reaches our heart, our compassion and understanding of emptiness transforms it into shining clear light. This streams back to all beings as we exhale. It shines over them and brings them every happiness. We do this as long as it feels comfortable.

When we finish the meditation, we wish that all the good just created may benefit all beings.

The goal of this meditation is to plant good impressions in one's mind in order to benefit others.

The Way Things Are

16TH KARMAPA MEDITATION

(The Main Guru Yoga Meditation
of Diamond Way Buddhism)

In the late 60s the 16th Karmapa Ranjung Rigpe Dorje made Hannah and me holders of this practical and comprehensive tool for enlightenment. Honoring his wish over the years that we always keep it fresh and on the cutting edge of Western minds, the focus of the meditation has shifted several times. Here the emphasis is on actively continuing the pure view obtained in meditation in our daily lives.

After taking refuge in the morning, you may informally and at any time during the day, let the Lama appear in front of you and receive his blessing. If unfamiliar with the form of Karmapa, one can equally visualize a golden buddha from. I know of no more effective meditation. Therefore, practice and enjoy.

We feel the formless stream of air at the tips of our noses, and let thoughts and feelings pass without evaluation.

The Four Thoughts

Then we focus on the four basic thoughts, which turn mind towards liberation and enlightenment:

We recognize our precious opportunity in this life, that we can benefit countless beings through the methods of a buddha. Few people ever meet Diamond Way teachings and even fewer are able to use them.

We remember the impermanence of everything composite. Only the unlimited clear space of mind is lasting and it is uncertain how long conditions will remain for recognizing it.

We understand causality, that it is up to us what will happen. Former thoughts, words, and actions became our present state and right now we are sowing the seeds for our future.

Finally, we see the reasons for working with mind. Enlightenment is timeless highest bliss and we cannot benefit others while confused or disturbed ourselves. Therefore we now open up to those who can teach us.

Refuge and the Enlightened Attitude

To bring all beings to enlightenment, we take Refuge:
In the *Buddha*, mind's full development,
In his *Teachings* which bring us there,
In the *Bodhisattvas*, our friends on the way,
And especially in the *Lama*, here the 16th Karmapa. He unites blessing, methods, and protection and is needed for our fast development.

Building Up Phase

Now out of space in front of us condenses the golden, transparent form of the 16th Karmapa, a radiant field of energy and light.

Karmapa wears the Black Crown, the shape of which can awaken mind's deepest awareness. His face is golden and mild. He sees us, knows us, and wishes us everything good. His hands hold a dorje and a bell crossed at his heart. They express the state of compassion and wisdom inseparable. Seated in meditation posture, he is surrounded by light.

Karmapa unites space and bliss and is the activity of all buddhas. His essence is here whether a clear image is perceived or not. We strongly wish to accomplish his enlightened qualities for the benefit of all.

Karmapa knows our wish. He smiles and comes ever closer through space. He now remains at a pleasant distance in front of us.

"Dearest Lama, essence of all buddhas, please show us the power which removes the ignorance and obscurations of all beings and ourselves. Let mind's timeless light be recognized inside us."

Blessing Phase – Body

A strong clear light radiates from between Karmapa's eyebrows and enters the same place in our forehead. Our head is filled with powerful clear light. The light dissolves all disturbing impressions in brain, nerves, and senses. All causes and imprints of harmful actions disappear and our body relaxes. It becomes a conscious tool for protecting and helping others. We retain the clear light for as long as we wish and experience the inner vibration of the syllable OM.

Pause

Blessing Phase — Speech

Emanating from Karmapa's throat, a radiant beam of red light streams out. It enters our mouth and throat. The light dissolves all difficulties in our speech. All impressions of harmful and confused words disappear and we become conscious of our speech. It is now compassion and wisdom, a powerful tool for benefiting others. Along with the red light, we retain the deep vibration of the syllable AH.

Pause

Blessing Phase — Mind

From the heart level in the center of Karmapa's transparent body, an intense blue light shines out. It fills the middle of our chest. Everything harmful now leaves our mind. Disturbing feelings and stiff ideas dissolve and our mind becomes spontaneous joy. It is space and bliss inseparable. Together with the deep blue light vibrates the syllable HUNG.

Pause

Great Seal Transmission

Now, all three lights enter us at the same time. Clear light fills our head, red light our throat, and blue light our heart center. Thus we obtain the essential state of the Great Seal.

Pause

We may now use the mantra KARMAPA CHENNO. It means power of all buddhas work through us. We repeat it loudly or inwardly.

Karmapa Chenno

Completion Phase

In front, Karmapa's golden form and his Black Crown dissolve into rainbow light. It falls on us, is everywhere, and all form disappears. There is now only awareness with no center or limit.

Pause

Whatever may appear is the free play of space.

Pause

Activity Phase

Now our surroundings, this world and all worlds appear, perfect and pure. Everything vibrates with joy and is kept together by love. All is fresh and meaningful, radiant with unlimited potential.

Beings manifest, near and far. They are female or male buddhas, whether they know it or not. Sounds are mantras and all thoughts wisdom, for the sole reason that they can happen.
We feel our own body condense out of space. It is power and joy. Something essential has happened. Before, we *were* our body and thus vulnerable to old age, sickness, death and loss. Now we *have* our body. Body and speech are conscious tools for benefiting others.

Our true essence, and we know that now, is the clear awareness just experienced. It was also present when there was no form.

We decide to keep this understanding in all life's situations and wish that the good impressions that just appeared become limitless. May they bring all beings the only lasting joy, that of knowing mind.

GLOSSARY

Accomplisher (Tibetan: *Naljorpa* (male), *Naljorma* (female), Sankrit: *Yogi* (male), *Yogini* (female): Buddhist practitioner who mainly focuses on realizing the nature of mind, independent of outer securities or societal conventions. In Asia Buddhists were monks, lay practitioners, or yogis. Today, due to the good general education in the West, the lifestyles and views of lay practitioners and of yogis have become more intermingled.

All Pervading Wisdom: Showing spontaneously arising insight. One of the Five Wisdoms represented by the white Buddha Radiant One (Tibetan: *Nampar Nangdze*, Sanskrit: *Vairochana*) of the Tathagata Buddha family. It corresponds with the element of space and the center. It appears through the transformation of ignorance.

Bell (Tibetan: *Trilbu*, Sanskrit: *Ghanta*): A ritual object used together with a dorje, symbolizing wisdom and space. On the level of the Diamond Way, together the bell and dorje denote the inseparability of space (female) and joy (male), wisdom and compassion.

Black Crown (Tibetan: *Shwa nag*): The special attribute of the Karmapas. In the moment of his enlightenment, Karmapa received the Black Crown. Woven from the wisdom hair of the dakinis, with it they crowned him Master of Buddha Activity. The crown is a powerfield that is constantly above Karmapa's head and visible to highly accomplished beings. During the Crown Ceremony he uses a replica of this crown. Seeing or meditating on the Black Crown causes an openness that allows one to purify the deepest levels of mind and to realize its nature. One can even reach liberation merely by seeing it.

Blessing: (1) A transmission of experience by a realized master. (2) Spiritual influence leading to the experience of the reduction of disturbing emotions. According to Tibetan texts blessings are a very effective way to transfer spiritual maturity.

Bodhgaya (also Bodh Gaya): The place in Northern India where the fourth historical Buddha, Shakyamuni Gautama, reached complete enlightenment approximately 2450 years ago. All 1,000 historical buddhas of this time period will manifest their full enlightenment here.

Bodhisattva (Sanskrit, Tibetan: *Changchub Sempa*): Someone who strives for enlightenment for the benefit of all beings without ever losing courage. This attitude corresponds to the ideal of the Great Way. On one hand a bodhisattva is someone who has understood emptiness and has developed compassion, and on the other hand the term is used for those who have taken the Bodhisattva Promise.

Bodhisattva Levels, Ten (Tibetan: *Sa chu*, Sanskrit: *Dasha bhumi*): According to the Great Way teachings there are ten levels of bodhisattva's development as one becomes a fully enlightened buddha. In each stage more subtle concepts are purified and a further degree of enlightened qualities manifest. The ten levels are: (1) The Joyful One, (2) The Stainless One, (3) The Illuminating One, (4) The Radiant One, (5) The One Difficult to Purify, (6) The Manifesting One, (7) The One Gone Afar, (8) The Immovable One, (9) The One with Excellent Wisdom, and (10) The Cloud of Dharma.

Bodhisattva Promise: The promise to accomplish buddhahood for the benefit of all beings and to work with diligence and strength, until all beings have reached enlightenment. It is taken in the presence of a realized bodhisattva and repeated in the context of daily meditation to strengthen this attitude.

Bond, Bonds (Tibetan: *Damtsig*, Sanskrit: *Samaya*): The basis for fast spiritual development in Diamond Way Buddhism. Through unbroken connections to the lama, to the buddha aspects and those with whom they received initiations and teachings, a practitioner quickly develops their inherent qualities.

Buddha (Sanskrit, Tibetan: *Sangye*) (1) Purified and fully developed. Denotes the enlightened state of mind. In Tibetan *sang* means completely purified of all veils that obscure the clarity of mind. *Gye* means complete development of all inherent qualities of mind including fearlessness, spontaneous joy and active compassion. (2) The Awakened One, in Sanskrit. The buddha of our age is the historical Buddha Shakyamuni, the fourth of 1,000 historical buddhas who will manifest in this eon. Every historical buddha introduces a new period of dharma.

Buddha Activities, Four: There are four buddha activities: pacifying, increasing, fascinating, and powerfully protecting. They describe brave, compassionate, spontaneous, and effortless behavior (the ability to do the right thing at the right place and time). Their basis is the ability to rest in that which is.

Buddha Families, Five (Tibetan: *Gyalwa rig nga*; Sanskrit: *Panca tathagata*): Also the Five Dhyani Buddhas. All buddha forms transmitted by the Buddha are categorized into the Five Buddha Families, which together represent full realization. The Five Disturbing Emotions are the raw materials which are transformed into the Five Wisdoms through meditation.

Buddha Form/ Buddha Aspect (Tibetan: *Yidam*; Sanskrit: *Istadevata*): One of the Three Roots. The limitless qualities of the enlightened mind express themselves in countless forms of energy and light. When one uses them in meditation and in daily life, they awaken the inherent buddha nature in everyone. They are seen as inseparable from one's own lama. In order to meditate on them, one needs the permission or the empowerment from a lama who holds their transmission.

Buddha Nature: The nature of mind, the potential in everyone to achieve buddhahood.

Buddha States, Four (Tibetan: *Ku sum*, Sanskrit: *Trikaya*): Also called the Three Buddha States. The Truth State (Sanskrit: *Dharmakaya*) is the insight into the ultimate empty essence of all appearances. It is connected to the experience of fearlessness. The Joy State (Sanskrit: *Sambhogakaya*) is connected to the experience of unconditioned joy. The Emanation State (Sanskrit: *Nirmanakaya*) is connected to the experience of unconditional compassion. The Essence State (Sanskrit: *Svabhabikaya*) is not an additional state, but rather the experience of the union of the Three Buddha States: the Truth State, the Joy State and the Emanation State. The Four Buddha States are transmitted in gomlungs (meditations guided by a teacher) and in empowerments.

Buddahood: Enlightenment

Building Up Phase (Tibetan: *Kye rim*, Sanskrit: *Utpatikrama*): Also called the Development Phase. Phase of a Diamond Way meditation where one mentally builds up or calls to mind a buddha aspect. It generates feelings of devotion and thankfulness, and solidifies itself as a trusting, deep, peaceful state of mind.

Calm Abiding (Tibetan: *Shiney*, Sanskrit: *Shamatha*): Also called Tranquil Mind. While meditating on an actual, representational, or abstract object, one tries to let the mind be one-pointed and dwell without distraction from the object. In both the Sutra Way and the Tantra Way, Calm Abiding is the foundation for recognizing the true nature of mind.

Center: Diamond Way Center

Chagchen (Tibetan) The Great Seal

Cheu (Tibetan) Dharma

Clarity (Tibetan: *Sal wa*, Sanskrit: *Vyakta*): Emptiness, clarity, and limitlessness are absolute qualities of mind that cannot be separated from one another. Clarity is mind's inherent ability to experience without interruption. Its realization is the manifestation of the Joy State.

Compassion (Tibetan: *Nyingje*, Sanskrit: *Karuna*): The second of the Four Immeasurables, the wish that all living beings may be free from suffering and the causes of suffering.

Completion Phase (Tibetan: *Dzog rim*, Sanskrit: *Sampanakrama*): Phase of a Diamond Way meditation that awakens mental abilities by melting together with a buddha aspect. A direct meditation on the nature of mind that leads to deep insight accomplished when form dissolves into awareness and one perceives the world and all beings as pure. Thoughts are then wisdom and sounds mantras.

Conscious Dying: Phowa

Dharma (Sanskrit, Tibetan: *Cheu*): Buddha's teachings. Translates literally as *the way things are*. Part of the Buddhist Refuge. It encompasses the three levels of teachings, the Small Way, Great Way, and Diamond Way, that the Buddha gave to his students according to their dispositions.

Dharmakaya (Sanskrit): Truth State

Diamond: Dorje

Diamond Mind (Tibetan: *Dorje Sempa*, Sanskrit: *Vajrasattva*): The buddha representing the purifying power of all buddhas. He is in the Joy State, white in color, and depicted sitting in either full meditation or the activity posture. His right hand holds a dorje to his heart and his left hand holds a bell at his hip.

Diamond Way (Tibetan: *Dorje thegpa*, Sanskrit: *Vajrayana*): Also called *Tantrayana* and *Mantrayana*. The highest level of Buddha's teachings, encompassing body, speech, and mind with a goal of full enlightenment. In this practice the goal also becomes the path by using fast methods which go deep. These teachings can only be used with the perspective of seeing everything as fundamentally pure.

Diamond Way Center: Buddhist center of the Karma Kagyu lineage founded and directed by Hannah and Lama Ole Nydahl, under the spiritual guidance of H.H. the 17th Karmapa Trinley Thaye Dorje. A place where people learn from Buddha's timeless wisdom, meditate, and share experience and development.

Discriminating Wisdom: Shows the world of appearances, all its details, and how they work together. One of the Five Wisdoms represented by the red Buddha of Limitless Light (Tibetan: *Opame*, Sanskrit: *Amitabha*) of the Lotus Family. It corresponds to the element of Fire and the direction West and appears through the transformation of attachment.

Dissolving Phase: Completion Phase

Disturbing Emotions (Tibetan: *Nyoen mong*, Sanskrit: *Klesha*): Also called mental states that bring about suffering. The states are ignorance, attachment, anger, pride, and jealousy. Together with negative actions, they form the causes for all suffering in the cycle of existence, Samsara.

Dorje (Tibetan, Sanskrit: *Vajra*): Translates as *king of stones and diamond*. A symbol of indestructibility and stability that characterizes the highest state of mind, enlightenment. Ritual object that symbolizes the methods of the Diamond Way. Shown with a bell, as joy, is a symbol of compassion.

Dzogchen (Tibetan): Great Perfection

Eightfold Path: Collection of the methods that lead to liberation mainly used in the Small Way. There are eight orienting points for human though, speech, and action that relate to the developing of wisdom, overcoming ignorance, acting meaningfully, and handling one's own consciousness.

Emanation State, The (Tibetan: *Tulku*, Sanskrit: *Nirmanakaya*): Also the Compassionate Emanation State. One of the Four Buddha States. The word tulku translates literally as *illusory body*. This state expresses the unobstructed ability of mind to manifest from space. In its highest meaning it refers to a historical buddha, a perfect tulku. The term can also refer to other forms of tulkus, such as expert tulkus or tulkus of good deeds, who, for example, act for the benefit of others as healers, artists, or scientists. There are also born tulkus, who, for example, can choose a birth as an animal, in order to help beings. There are tulkus who can clearly recall previous lives and others who can barely remember them at all. Tulkus show themselves in order to make the access to buddha nature possible for beings. Tulkus do not feel they *are* their body, rather that they *have* their body, and use them as tools for the benefit of all beings.

Empowerment (Tibetan: *Wang*, Sanskrit: *Abisheka*): Also called *initiation*. The introduction of a practitioner into the power-field of a buddha form, most often connected with ceremonies, where a student receives an empowerment to meditate on that form.

Practice empowerments are connected with promises. Empowerments can also be given as blessings, also called permission empowerments. Here one makes a bond with the lama, and obstacles on the way to enlightenment are purified. For Diamond Way practice, the oral transmission (Tibetan: *Lung*) and instructions (Tibetan: *Tri*) are necessary, along with the empowerment. The more immediate way of a guided meditation in one's own language (Tibetan: *Gomlung*), accomplishes the same goals. In the Kagyu lineage, the meditation on the teacher (Guru Yoga) is most important. All buddha forms are experienced as inseparable from the teacher.

Emptiness (Tibetan: *Tongpanyi*, Sanskrit: *Shunyata*): Emptiness, clarity, and limitlessness are absolute qualities of mind that cannot be separated from one another. Empty of independent existence, nothing arises by itself, but rather is dependent upon conditions. Emptiness is the final nature of all outer and inner phenomena and cannot be grasped through concepts. Its realization is the manifestation of the Truth State.

Enlightened Attitude: Enlightened mind

Enlightened Mind (Tibetan: *Chang chub kyi sem*, Sanskrit: *Bodhicitta*): The wish to reach enlightenment for the good of all beings is the basis for the Great Way and the Diamond Way. The enlightened mind has two aspects: the conditioned or relative and the absolute. In the conditioned aspect, enlightened mind consists of the wish accompanied by perfecting oneself through the Six Liberating Actions for the benefit of all beings. The ultimate or absolute enlightened mind recognizes the inseparability of emptiness and compassion. This leads to spontaneous and effortless activity which is beyond any concept or hesitation, as subject, object, and action are no longer experienced as separate from each other. The enlightened mind is the attitude of a bodhisattva, the Enlightened Attitude.

Enlightenment, Enlightened: The full development of mind, buddahood, the state of a Buddha.

Equalizing Wisdom: Shows the conditioned nature of all things, that nothing has a self-nature and therefore actually everything is equal. One of the Five Wisdoms represented by the Buddha Jewel Born (Tibetan: *Rinchen Jungden*, Sanskrit: *Ratnasambhava*) of the Jewel Family. It corresponds to the element of Earth and the direction of South. It appears through the transformation of pride.

Equanimity (Tibetan: *Tang nyom*, Sanskrit: *Upeksha*): The fourth of the Four Immeasurables, means to remain free from attachment and aversion in a balanced and benevolent state of mind.

Essence/Essential State, The (Tibetan: *Ngowo nyi ku*, Sanskrit: *Svabhabikakaya*): Not an individual state but the experience of the inseparable union of the Three Buddha States: the Truth, Joy, and Emanation States. One of the Four Buddha States.

Form states: The Joy State and the Emanation State. They arise from the Truth State and bring benefit to others.

Foundational Practices, Four (Tibetan: Chagchen *Ngondro*): The preparation for the Great Seal, also named the Four Special Preliminaries. With the Foundational Practices one creates countless good impressions in the subconscious. They build the foundation for the Great Seal. With each of these practices there are 111,111 repetitions. These mediations are: (1) *Taking Refuge and Developing the Enlightened Attitude* through prostrations (2) Purifying the impressions that bring suffering through the *Diamond Mind Meditation* (3) Offering good impressions with *Mandala Offerings* (4) *Meditation on the Lama* (*Guru Yoga*).

Four Basic Thoughts, The (Tibetan: _Lodro nam shi_): The four things that turn the mind are also named the Four Ordinary Preliminaries. Four thoughts that develop a deep understanding of the basic facts of our lives and direct mind towards the Dharma. These thoughts are: (1) The precious opportunity of our current existence to encounter the teachings which lead to liberation and enlightenment. (2) Impermanence. Since all conditions are understood to be in constant change, one should use every opportunity to recognize mind. (3) Karma, cause and effect that shapes one's life with one's thoughts, words, and actions. (4) The disadvantage of conditioned existence where enlightenment is the only true and lasting joy.

Four Immeasurables, The (Tibetan: _Tse me shi_, Sanskrit: _A pramana_): Often expressed by four wishes: (1) May all beings have happiness and the cause of happiness. (2) May they be without suffering and the cause of suffering. (3) May they never be without the highest joy, which is completely without suffering. (4) May they rest in equanimity free from attachment and aversion. Love is the wish that others are happy. Compassion is the wish that others are free from suffering. Sympathetic joy is rejoicing in the positive actions of others and the wish for their lasting happiness. Equanimity means to rest in a balanced and benevolent state of mind free from aversion and attachment.

Four main/major schools/lineages of Tibetan Buddhism: Kagyu, Nyingma, Sakya, and Gelug.

Gampopa (1079-1153): Milarepa's main student and teacher of the first Karmapa, Duesum Khyenpa. The Buddha prophesized that Gampopa would spread the Dharma all across Tibet. He united the Kadampa School of Atisha with the way of the Great Seal. The monastic stream of the Kagyu lineage begins with him. He said of his philosophical masterpiece, _The Jewel Ornament of Liberation_, that to read it would be the same as meeting him. This book explains the views and path of the Great Way and is an excellent introduction to the foundations of Buddhism.

Gelugpas (Tibetan), Gelug lineage, Gelug school: Two possible translations: the Virtuous School or the Ganden School, named after their main monastery. They are also called the Yellow Hat school, the newest of the four main lineages of Tibetan Buddhism. This reformed school, first founded in the 14th century by Tsongkhapa, especially stresses the textual studies as well as the monastic tradition. Although this school also possesses various tantric transmissions, they mainly see themselves as Great Way rather than Diamond Way.

Gomlung (Tibetan): Guided meditation

Great Middle Way, The (Tibetan: *Uma Chenpo*, Sanskrit: *Maha Madhyamaka*): Philosophical view of the Great Way which overcomes all extreme opinions like the acceptance of things as real and the idea that they are not. Based on the Buddha's Perfection of Wisdom (Sanskrit: *Prajnaparamita*) teachings. These teachings were expounded by the Indian master Nagarjuna and other later masters.

Great Perfection, The (Tibetan: *Dzogchen* and *Dzogpa chenpo*, Sanskrit: *Maha ati*): The ultimate teaching of the Nyingma or Old School. Its essence and goal correspond to the Great Seal of the Kagyu transmission. However, the methods and path are different.

Great Seal, The (Tibetan: *Chagchen* and *Chagya chenpo*, Sanskrit: *Mahamudra*): The Great Seal of realization. Buddha promised that this is the ultimate teaching. It is mainly taught in the Kagyu school and leads to a direct experience of the nature of mind. The Great Seal encompasses the basis, way, and goal.

With trust in one's buddha nature, one tries to rest in the inseparability of the experiencer, that which is being experienced, and the experience itself. As a result, mind recognizes itself and seals its enlightenment.

Great Way (Tibetan: *Thegchen*, Sanskrit: *Mahayana*): The way of the bodhisattvas where one strives for enlightenment for the benefit of all beings. Compassion and wisdom are deepened through study, analysis, and meditation over a long time, and then open out into insight.

Guided Meditation (Tibetan: *Gomlung*): Translates as meditation reading of a text. Common way in which meditations are taught in Diamond Way Buddhist centers. A breakthrough in the transmission of Buddhism in the West.

Guru (Sanskrit): Lama

Guru Rinpoche (Tibetan: *Pema Jungne*, Sanskrit: *Padmasambhava*): The Lotus Born. Brought Buddhism, in particular the Diamond Way transmissions, to Tibet in the eighth century. He led an exciting life and performed innumerable miracles. With his termas and his prophecies of the tertons, he founded the Nyingma lineage. He is also highly esteemed by the Kagyus and the Sakyas.

Guru Yoga (Sanskrit, Tibetan: *Lami Naljor*): Meditation on the teacher (Lama) as the essence of all buddhas. Through this practice, just as in an *empowerment*, one receives the blessing of the lama's body, speech, and mind; and the Four Buddha States are awakened. In the practice one melts together and identifies with the enlightened essence of the lama.

Hinayana: Small Way

Initiation: Empowerment

Insight (Tibetan: *Lhaktong*, Sanskrit: *Vipassana*): Also Penetrating Insight. This meditation practice is used as a method in the Sutra Way as well as in the Tantra Way and builds on a stable Calm Abiding experience. One tries to maintain from moment to moment the view of the non-duality of perceiving consciousness and perceived objects. There is an analytical and a direct approach.

Instructions (Tibetan: *Tri*, related to Sanskrit: *Upadesha*): Practical explanation of how to meditate, given by a lama or in many cases also by an experienced student.

Invocation: Short spoken or written meditation on a buddha aspect to evoke his powerfield and to experience the qualities embodied by it in one's own development.

Joy: Also space. Buddhism distinguishes between conditioned and unconditioned joy. Conditioned joy arises from composite, and therefore impermanent, conditions. Unconditioned joy is the realization of the nature of mind which is beyond the duality of joyful and non-joyful states. Once one has fully recognized unconditioned joy the realization stays, it is unchanged by outer conditions. It is always fresh and unaffected by conditioned happiness and suffering.

Joy State, The (Tibetan: *Long ku*, Sanskrit: *Sambhogakaya*): Body of perfect enjoyment, one of the Four Buddha States. The enlightened expression of the clarity of mind, its free play, and the experience of highest joy. This state is experienced when mind recognizes its rich possibilities on the level of fearlessness. It manifests from the Truth State as various buddha forms and their powerfields. Advanced bodhisattvas can encounter these forms and receive blessings, acknowledgement, as well as direct insight.

Kagyupas, Kagyu lineage, Kagyu school: The accomplisher transmission within the four main schools of Tibetan Buddhism. It encompasses the old (Tibetan: *Nyingma*) and new (Tibetan: *Sarma*) teachings that reached Tibet. Being heavily practice oriented, it is sometimes called the School of Oral Transmission. It was brought to Tibet around 1050 by the hero Marpa and draws its strength from the close relationship between teacher and student. Four major and eight minor schools have their origin in the four main students of Gampopa. *Major* and *minor* relate to the direct connection to Gampopa (major or main schools) or indirect connection through a student of Gampopa (minor or subsidiary schools). Today out of the major schools, only the Karma Kagyu is left, whose spiritual leader is the Karmapa. From the eight minor schools the Drugpa and Drikung Kagyu have many supporters in Bhutan and Ladakh.

Kangyur (Tibetan): Translation of the Buddha's words. A collection of the direct teachings of the Buddha. 100, 103, 106, or 108 volumes, depending on the edition.

Karma (Sanskrit, Tibetan: *Ley*): Action. The law of cause and effect, according to which one experiences the world in line with the impressions stored in mind, created through one's actions of body, speech, and mind. This means that one decide one's own future with one's present actions.

Karmapa (Tibetan): One who carries out the activity of all buddhas or master of buddha activity. The first consciously reincarnated lama of Tibet and spiritual leader of the Karma Kagyu lineage since the 12th century. The Karmapa embodies the activity of all buddhas and was predicted by Buddha Shakyamuni and Guru Rinpoche. Before their deaths many Karmapas left a letter that described the exact circumstances of their next birth. Until today there have been 17 incarnations
(1) Duesum Khyenpa, 1110 – 1193

(2) Karma Pakshi, 1204 – 1283

(3) Rangjung Dorje, 1284 – 1339

(4) Roelpe Dorje, 1340 – 1383

(5) Deshin Shegpa, 1384 – 1415

(6) Tongwa Doenden, 1416 – 1453

(7) Choedrak Gyamtso, 1454 – 1506

(8) Mikyoe Dorje, 1507 – 1554

(9) Wangchug Dorje, 1556 – 1603

(10) Choying Dorje, 1604 – 1674

(11) Yeshe Dorje, 1676 – 1702

(12) Changchub Dorje, 1703 – 1732

(13) Duedul Dorje, 1733 – 1797

(14) Thegchog Dorje, 1798 – 1868

(15) Khakhyab Dorje, 1871 – 1922

(16) Rangjung Rigpe Dorje, 1924 – 1981

(17) Trinley Thaye Dorje, 1983 – present.

Lama (Tibetan, Sanskrit: *Guru*): The highest or heavy with good qualities. Buddhist teacher. One of the Three Roots. He is especially important in the Diamond Way as he is the key to the deepest teachings. Through the Guru Yoga meditation on the lama, one receives his blessing, through which one may momentarily experience the true nature of mind. The lama mirrors the Three States of Enlightenment.

Lhaktong (Tibetan, Sankrit: *Vipassana*): Insight

Liberating Actions, Six (Tibetan: *Parole tu jinpa druk*, Sanskrit: *Sat Parimita*): Liberating actions of the bodhisattvas. Most often the following six are mentioned: Generosity, meaningful lifestyle, patience, joyful effort, meditation, and liberating wisdom.

Liberation/liberated: Release from the cycle of existence (Sanskrit: *Samsara*), the state of mind in which all suffering and the causes for suffering are completely overcome. It happens through dissolving the false idea of a presumed *I*. On this level all disturbing emotions fall away. When the last stiff concepts are also let go, then one becomes enlightened.

Limitlessness (Tibetan: *Mangapa*, Sanskrit: *Niruddha*): Emptiness, clarity, and limitlessness are absolute qualities of mind that cannot be separated from one another. Describes the fact that buddha activity manifests out of space unimpeded, spontaneously and without effort. Its realization is the manifestation of the Emanation State.

Lopon Tsechu Rinpoche (1918-2003): Great master of Diamond Way Buddhism, born in the Kingdom of Bhutan. He received full dharma training in Nepal and meditated under severe conditions in the caves of Milarepa and in the holy places of Guru Rinpoche. A close disciple of the 16th Karmapa and the first teacher of Hannah and Lama Ole Nydahl. A highly respected teacher in the East and a major inspiration in the establishment of Diamond Way Buddhism in the West. He oversaw the building of many important stupas in Europe and Asia.

Love (Tibetan: *Jampa*, Sanskrit: *Maitri*): The first of the Four Immeasurables. The wish that all are happy and have the causes of happiness.

Loving Eyes (Tibetan: Chenrezig, Sanskrit: Avalokiteshvara): Buddha of compassion and of non-discriminating love. He is in the Joy State, white in color, seated in full meditation posture. He has four arms; his outer right hand holds a crystal mala, which frees all beings from the conditioned world. Both of his middle hands hold the jewel of enlightenment in front of his heart. His outer left hand holds a lotus blossom, which shows the purity of his view. His eyes see all beings.

Lung (Tibetan): Oral transmission

Maha Ati (Sanskrit): Great Perfection

Mahamudra (Sanskrit): Great Seal

Mahayana (Sanskrit): Great Way

Maitripa (1007-1088): Maitripa was a student of Naropa and later became one of Marpa's main teachers. He showed miracles and lived the life of a Mahasiddha. His main activity was the transmission of the teachings of the Great Seal of the Kagyu school. Countless meditations that are still practiced today in ways that are suitable for daily life go back to Maitripa, the meditations of the Way of Insight.

Mandala (Sanskrit, Tibetan: *Khyilkhor*): Center and surroundings. (1) The powerfield of a buddha, which emerges out of the countless possibilities of space or the depiction thereof. In a broader sense, the powerfield of a person or a group. (2) Mentally presented universe filled with the precious things that one offers to the buddhas when doing the Mandala Offerings meditation, the third part of the Four Foundational Practices. (3) The metal disk that is used in the Mandala Offerings meditation.

Mantra (Sanskrit, Tibetan: *Ngag*): Natural vibration of a buddha form. Reciting a mantra activates the buddha form's powerfield. Many Diamond Way meditations have a phase where mantras are repeated.

Mantra Way: Mantrayana

Mantrayana (Sanskrit): Tantra

Marpa (1012-1097): The Great Translator, he traveled three times from Tibet to India where he spent sixteen years learning from his teachers. He was instrumental in reestablishing Buddhism in Tibet after it had declined. His main teachers were Naropa and Maitripa. From them he received the Six Teachings of Naropa and the teachings on the Great Seal. He was the first Tibetan lineage holder of the Kagyu school and was the teacher of Milarepa. The transmission for lay people and yogis is often called Marpa Kagyu. Monks and nuns in the Kagyu lineage follow the Dhagpo Kagyu path of Gampopa.

Meditation, Buddhist (Tibetan: *Gom*): The Tibetan word *gom* means become familiar with and expresses a process in which mind tries to let go of its veils. For this, one uses methods that bring what is understood intellectually into one's own experience. On the highest level, meditation means to effortlessly remain in that which is. On the various levels of Buddha's teachings different methods are taught, but they can be summarized essentially as Calm Abiding and Insight. In the Diamond Way the most important methods are identification with enlightenment, awakening the enlightened powerfield using mantras, gratitude, and holding the pure view. Just as it was earlier in Tibet, in the caves of the accomplishers, so today in the West, guided meditation (Tibetan: *Gomlung*) enables a large number of people to gain access to the countless methods of the Diamond Way.

Meditation on the 16th Karmapa, 16th Karmapa Meditation: This meditation was given by the 16th Karmapa. It is a form of Guru Yoga and is used in the Diamond Way Buddhist centers of the Karma Kagyu lineage as the main practice for public meditation sessions.

Melting Phase: Completion Phase

Milarepa (1040-1123): The main student of Marpa and the teacher of Gampopa. He is the most well known of the Tibetan accomplishers and is revered by all Tibetan lineages. After he took revenge on and killed thirty five enemies of his family, following his mother's wishes, he sought a way to purify all the bad karma that he had accumulated. He met Marpa and grounded in his unshakeable confidence in Marpa and in his own will, continued to meditate under the most difficult conditions, reaching enlightenment in one lifetime.

Mind: Experienced as the habitual stream of physical and mental impressions. In its unenlightened state it expresses its ability to think, perceive and remember through the consciousness. Its true enlightened nature is free of any self-centeredness and perceives itself as not separate from space as indestructible, limitless awareness. The recognition of its nature leads to fearlessness, self-arisen love and active compassion.

Mirrorlike Wisdom: Shows the way things are without adding or subtracting anything. One of the Five Wisdoms, represented by the blue Buddha Unshakeable (Tibetan: *Mikyoepa*, Sanskrit: *Akshobya*) of the Diamond Family. Corresponds to the element of Water and the direction East. It appears through the transformation of anger.

Naropa (956-1040): Student of Tilopa and teacher of Marpa. Indian Mahasiddha and earlier a scholar of Nalanda University, one of the great Buddhist universities in India. After eight years he resigned from academic life and became a wandering accomplisher, seeking his true teacher. He authored the first written compendium of the important tantric teachings, the *Six Teachings of Naropa*.

Nature of Mind: Buddha nature

Ngondro (Tibetan): Four Foundational Practices

Nirmanakaya (Sanskrit): Emanation State

Nirvana (Sanskrit, Tibetan: *Nyang ngen le depa*): The state beyond suffering. In general, liberation from suffering in samsara. Specifically in the Great Way, the state of perfect buddhahood. The non-clinging or Great Nirvana, meaning *to rest in that which is.* In this state, if nothing happens, it is the space of mind. If something happens, it is the free play of mind. If nothing appears, it is mind's space essence. If something appears, be it outer or inner, it is mind's free play. And the fact that all experiences can appear mind's unlimited expression.

Nyingmapas, Nyingma lineage, Nyingma school: The oldest of the four main lineages of Tibetan Buddhism. It was founded in the eighth century by the Indian master Guru Rinpoche. There is a distinction between the Kama tradition (the school of direct transmission from teacher to student, which goes all the way back to Buddha Shakyamuni) and the Terma tradition, the transmission of hidden treasures which were rediscovered and propagated later. In the year 800 King Langdarma turned against Buddhism and destroyed these transmission lineages. But the tertons (treasure finders) rediscovered the teachings of Guru Rinpoche for us today. Many tertons were once Kagyus, and in sharing the transmissions a close connection developed between the Kagyu and the Nyingma schools.

Oh Diamond (Tibetan: *Kye Dorje*, Sanskrit: *Hevajra*): The central buddha aspect of the Sakya lineage, and the main yidam practice of Marpa. He is in the Joy State, blue in color, and is often depicted standing in union with his consort No-Self (Tibetan: *Dagmema*, Sanskrit: *Nairatmya*), also the name of Marpa's wife. His appearance is half peaceful, half powerfully-protective, usually with eight heads and sixteen arms holding skull bowls, in which are animals on the right and gods on the left. He is adorned with powerfully protective ornaments such as a necklace of skulls and a tiger skin loincloth.

Oral Transmission (Tibetan: _Lung_, Sanskrit: _Agama_): Also oral authorization or reading of text. Ritual reading or recitation of a Diamond Way text, simply hearing the syllables transmits their inner meaning. An empowerment.

Paramitas, Six (Sanskrit:): Six Liberating Actions

Phowa (Tibetan, Sanskrit: _Samkranti_): Transference of Consciousness. Meditation of conscious dying. With this practice one prepares oneself for death later on. The result of successful practice is that one experiences a lot less fear and, upon death, goes to the Pure Land of Highest Joy.

Pointing-out instructions (Tibetan: _Sem tri_) Literally mind teaching or teachings on the nature of mind.

Powerfield: Mandala

Protector (Tibetan: _Cheukyong_, Sanskrit: _Dharmapala_): One of the Three Roots. They remove obstacles on the path to enlightenment and make every experience into a step of the way. Protectors, the source of buddha activity, are along with the yidams expressions of the Joy State and are essentially inseparable from the lama. In the Kagyu lineage, Black Coat (Tibetan: _Bernagchen_, Sanskrit: _Mahakala_) and Radiant Goddess (Tibetan: _Palden Lhamo_, Sanskrit: _Shri Devi_) are the most important protectors.

Pure Land: The powerfield of a Buddha. The most well known pure land is the Pure Land of Highest Joy of the Buddha of Limitless Light (Tibetan: _Dewachen_).

Pure Land of Highest Joy (Tibetan: _Dewachen_, Sanskrit: _Sukhavati_): The pure land of the Buddha of Limitless Light is particularly easy to reach through practices on the Buddha of

Limitless Light, including Phowa. When the false notion of an ego is dissolved on this level of awareness, it is only a matter of time until one reaches enlightenment.

Pure View: The view in the Diamond Way. One practices seeing the world and all beings as the self liberating play of space.

Purification: Generally, every Buddhist practice removes disturbing tendencies and impressions. As mind can enlighten itself out of a pleasant but not a disturbed state of mind, this step in work is unavoidable.

Radiance: The deeply convincing bliss which radiates from realization.

Rebirth: Reincarnation

Red Hat schools: Refers to the three old or tantric schools of Tibetan Buddhism: Kagyu, Nyingma, and Sakya. Named for the color of their ritual hats.

Red Wisdom (Tibetan: *Dorje Phamo*, Sanskrit: *Vajravarahi*): Diamond Sow. Female buddha aspect embodying the highest wisdom of all buddhas. She is depicted in the Joy State in a joyfully dancing form. She holds a chopping knife with her raised right hand and her left hand holds a skull bowl at her heart. Her form in union with Highest Joy (Tibetan: *Demchock*) is the most important yidam of the Kagyu lineage. Other important forms of Red Wisdom are Diamond Yogini (Tibetan: *Dorje naljorma*, Sanskrit: *Vajrayogini*) and Wisdom Dakini (Tibetan: *Yeshe Khandro*, Sanskrit: *Jnana dakini*).

Refuge (Tibetan: *Khyab dro*, Sanskrit: *Sharanam gam*): Translates literally as *go to protection*. Encountering one's own buddha nature, one turns to the values on which one can rely. One takes

Refuge in Buddha as the goal, in the Dharma as the way, and in the Sangha, the Bodhisattvas, as one's friends and helpers on the way. These are the so-called Three Jewels. In the Diamond Way one also takes refuge in the Three Roots. Receiving refuge from a lama is the ritual beginning of one's way. It creates a connection between the buddha nature of the student and the timeless wisdom of all buddhas. As a good sign, one gets a Buddhist name and a tiny bit of hair is cut. This reminds one that the Buddha, after he left his homeland and caste and decided to dedicate all his time and energy to enlightenment, cut his hair.

Reincarnation/Rebirth: Embodiment in a subsequent life. The same person is not reborn but the mind follows its unenlightened habit to think that things are real. It consolidates itself in a new life according to the karma which has been built up through actions, words and thoughts and this mind experiences a new world accordingly. Normally a reincarnation happens involuntarily but can also happen consciously on the basis of good wishes for the benefit of beings, if the nature of mind has been recognized and to a great extent.

Retreat, Buddhist: Meditating for days, weeks, or years in a quiet and isolated place, not being distracted by the entanglements of life. Most effective if one has a clear goal and a daily schedule, under the guidance of a Buddhist teacher. There are open and closed retreats for individuals, couples and groups. Times of withdrawal create more distance to the experiences of everyday life and deepen meditation experience.

Rinpoche (Tibetan): The Precious One. Title of respect, often given to Buddhist lamas.

Sakyapas, Sakya lineage, Sakya school: One of the four main schools of Tibetan Buddhism, founded by Khoen Koenchok Gyalpo in the eleventh century. In this school weight is given to both intellectual study and meditation practice.

Sambhogakaya (Sanskrit): Joy State

Samsara (Sanskrit, Tibetan: *Khorwa*): Cycle of existence. Involuntary reincarnation in conditioned states, also failing to master the world of experience.

Sangha (Sanskrit, Tibetan: *Gendun*): The community of practitioners, often used to designate a Buddhist group. As part of Buddhist Refuge, indicates the realized friends on the way.

Shiney (Tibetan): Calm Abiding

Six Energy Practices of Naropa (Tibetan: *Naro cheu druk*): Also the Six Teachings of Naropa. The very effective methods of the Kagyu lineage, only practiced in retreat. Their goal is the recognition of the nature of mind by means of its energy aspects. They include the following meditations: Inner Heat (Tibetan: *Tummo*, Sanskrit: *Chandali*), Clear Light (Tibetan: *Oesal*, Sanskrit: *Prabhabhava*), Dream (Tibetan: *Milam*, Sanskrit: *Svapnadarshana*), Illusory Body (Tibetan: *Gyulue*, Sanskrit: *Mayakaya*), Intermediate State (Tibetan: *Bardo*, Sanskrit: *Antarabhava*), and Transference of Consciousness or Conscious Dying (Tibetan: *Phowa*, Sanskrit: *Samkranti*).

Six Paramitas (Sanskrit:): Six Liberating Actions

Small Way (Tibetan: *Thek chung*, Sanskrit: *Hinayana*): The way of the Arhats, or listeners (Tibetan: *Nyenthoe*, Sanskrit: *Shravakas*) and individual buddhas or solitary realizers (Tibetan: *Rang sangye*, Sanskrit: *Pratyekabuddhas*). Here the focus is on one's own liberation.

Space: Timeless and present everywhere as the inherent potential of mind in everything, it contains knowledge, experiences joy, and expresses itself as meaningful and loving. Constantly realizing this space in and around oneself is full enlightenment. It is often misunderstood as a nothingness, something missing, or a black hole. However, it connects everything. Described by Buddha as emptiness, space encompasses and realizes all times and directions.

Store Consciousness (Tibetan: *Kun shi*, Sanskrit: *Alaya*): The aspect of consciousness that is the basis for the arising of all karmic imprints. A function of mind. The mind keeps positive, negative or neutral impressions and when corresponding conditions appear they begin to mature and manifest outwardly. Can be compared to the hard-drive memory of a computer.

Stupa (Sanskrit, Tibetan: *Cheurten*): A form, often a construction, which symbolizes perfect enlightenment, usually filled with relics and written mantras. Translated from the Tibetan, *cheur* means gifts and *ten* means foundation for offering gifts (of body, speech, and mind) to enlightenment. Buddha gave teachings on stupas in the Sutra of Dependent Arising. It represents the transformation of all emotions and elements into the Five Wisdoms and the Five Buddha Families. It is used by Buddhists as a site for making beyond personal wishes for the benefit of all beings and is circumambulated in clockwise direction. Often used as symbol representing the Sangha.

Sutra(s) (Sanskrit, Tibetan: *Do*): (1) Often called the Causal Way. For a long time one establishes the causes for enlightenment to recognize the characteristics of all things, their emptiness. Another name is Sutra Way (Tibetan: *Do yi thegpa*, Sanskrit: *Sutrayana*), one of the two subdivisions of the Great Way, which follows the causal methods given in the sutras. (2) Pathway. The sutras are the individual teachings of the Buddha, for example: The Heart Sutra.

Svabhabikakaya (Sanskrit): Essence/Essential State

Sympathetic Joy (Tibetan: *Ga wa*, Sanskrit: *Mudita*): The third of The Four Immeasurables, rejoicing in the useful actions of others and the wish that others may experience lasting happiness.

Tantra, Tantric, Buddhist (Sanskrit): (1) The path in which identification with enlightenment and holding the pure view are the most important methods. Based on the compassion and wisdom of the *Great Way*. Tantra Way (Tibetan: *Gyu kyi thegpa*, Sanskrit: *Tantrayana*) and Mantra Way (Tibetan: *Ngak gi thegpa*, Sanskrit: *Mantrayana*) are other names for Diamond Way (Tibetan: *Dorje thegpa*: Sanskrit: *Vajrayana*). Tantra Way is one of the two subdivisions of the *Great Way*, which follows the resultant methods given in the tantras. The goal, buddhahood, becomes the way. A fast way to enlightenment, prerequisites are: pure view, confidence in one's own mind and in one's lama, and a compassionate and courageous attitude (Enlightened Mind). (2) The tantras are the individual teachings given the Buddha on the Diamond Way level, e.g. the Tantra of the Buddha of Highest Bliss (Sanskrit: *Chakrasamvara Tantra*).

Tantrayana (Sanskrit): Tantra

Tengyur (Tibetan): Translation of the Treatises. The collection of the commentaries of the Indian masters on the teachings of the Buddha (Kangyur), between 225 and 256 volumes, depending on the edition.

Three Jewels (Tibetan: *Kon chog sum*, Sanskrit: *Triratna*): Buddha, Dharma, and Sangha. All Buddhists worldwide take refuge in them.

Three Roots (Tibetan: *Tsawa sum*, Sanskrit: *Trimula*): Lama, Yidam, and Protector. Above and beyond the Three Jewels, they are the Refuge in the Diamond Way and make possible a fast track to enlightenment. They are the source or roots of blessing, realization, and protection.

Three Year Retreat: Traditional training of many lamas in Tibetan Buddhism. It lasts three years, three months and three days. It is conducted in single sex groups. It consists of the Four Foundational Practices, outer, inner and secret yidam practices, and the Six Teachings of Naropa.

Tonglen (Tibetan): Translates as *giving and taking*. Meditation of the Great Way.

Tri (Tibetan): Meditation instructions

Truth State, The (Tibetan: *Cheuku*, Sanskrit: *Dharmakaya*): Body of phenomena. One of the Four Buddha States. The Truth State is timeless enlightenment as such, the empty nature of mind. It is the foundation for the Joy State and the Emanation State. It is the ultimate nature of a buddha, beyond all forms, characteristics, and limits. Recognition of the Truth State helps oneself and yields absolute fearlessness, whereas the Joy State and the Emanation State are for the sake of others.

Tulku (Tibetan, Sanskrit: Nirmanakaya): Emanation State.

Vajrayana (Sanskrit): Diamond Way

Veil (Tibetan: *Dribpa*, Sanskrit: *Avarana*): Unclear concepts or experiences which stand in the way of mind's experience of the world. Veils are based on ignorance and arise through disturbing emotions and extreme views.

View (Tibetan: *Ta wa*, Sanskrit: *Drsti*): The necessary knowledge that one needs in Buddhism for a meaningful life and productive meditation. Corresponds to the philosophical basis which is taught in one or more of the four philosophical schools of Buddhism.

Wang (Tibetan): Empowerment

Wheel of Life/Wheel of Existence (Tibetan: *Sipai khorlo*, Sanskrit: *Bhavachakra*): Pictorial representation of samsara as a wheel. The three poisons ignorance, attachment, and anger are represented respectively by a pig, a cockerel, and snake and appear at the hub of the wheel. The six realms, paranoia states, hungry ghost states, the realm of animals, the human realm, god, and half-god states appear between the spokes. The Twelve Links of Dependent Arising are around the rim. The wheel is held in the teeth of Yama, the Lord of Death, representing impermanence. Only the Buddha stands outside the wheel. This wheel is often found painted outside the entrance to traditional Buddhist temples in the Himalayas.

Wisdoms: Five Wisdoms

Wisdom of Experience: Showing developments in the phenomenal world. One of the Five Wisdoms represented by the green Buddha Meaningful Accomplishment (Tibetan: *Donyoe Drubpa*, Sanskrit: *Amogashiddhi*) of the Sword Buddha Family. Corresponds with the element of Air, with movement, and the direction of North. It appears through the transformation of jealousy.

Wisdoms, Five: The Five Wisdoms are the true essence of the Five Disturbing Emotions. Through the transformation of ordinary experience, anger is recognized as a mirror-like state, showing the way things are without adding or subtracting anything (Mirror-like

Wisdom). Pride becomes the ability to see all things as richness (Equalizing Wisdom). Attachment transforms into the capacity to distinguish things in their details and how they work together (Discriminating Wisdom). Jealousy transforms itself into the ability to connect experiences as steps in a historical process (Wisdom of Experience) and ignorance becomes all-pervading insight (All Pervading Wisdom).

Yellow Hat school: Gelugpa school, so-called because of the color of their ritual hats.

Yidam (Tibetan): Buddha form. One of the Three Roots. Source of enlightened qualities.

DIAMOND WAY BUDDHIST CENTERS WORLDWIDE

A Selection of Buddhist Centers of the Karma Kagyu Lineage under the spiritual guidance of the 17th Karmapa Trinley Thaye Dorje and directed by Lama Ole Nydahl.

Websites

International: http://www.diamondway-buddhism.org
Europe Center: http//www.europecenter.org
United States: http://www.diamondway.org
Canada: http://www.diamondway-buddhism.ca
United Kingdom: http://dwbuk.org
Australia: http://www.diamondway.org.au
New Zealand: http://www.diamondway-buddhism.org.nz

Centers

Australia

Buddhist Center Perth
+61 (8) 93991880
Perth@diamondway-center.org
www.diamondway.org.au/centres/perth/

Buddhist Center Sydney
+61 (2) 95655331
Sydney@diamondway-center.org
www.diamondway.org.au/centres/sydney/

Canada

Buddhist Center Calgary
+1 (403) 2558423
Calgary@diamondway-center.org
www.diamondway.org/calgary

Buddhist Center Edmonton
+1 (780) 4555488
Edmonton@diamondway-center.org
www.diamondway.org/edmonton

Buddhist Group Toronto
+1 (416) 8404575
Toronto@diamondway-center.org
www.diamondway.org/toronto

New Zealand

Buddhist Center Christchurch
+64 (3) 3813108
Christchurch@diamondway-center.org
www.diamondway-buddhism.org.nz

United Kingdom

Buddhist Center Liverpool
+44 (151) 2223543
Liverpool@diamondway-center.org
liverpool.dwbuk.org

Buddhist Center London
+44 (20) 79162282
London@diamondway-center.org
www.buddhism-london.org

United States of America
Buddhist Group Albuquerque
+1 (505) 256 3054
Albuquerque@diamondway-center.org
www.diamondway.org/albuquerque

Buddhist Center Austin
+1 (512) 371 9803
Austin@diamondway-center.org
www.diamondway.org/austin

Buddhist Center Chicago
+1 (312) 421 0133
Chicago@diamondway-center.org
www.diamondway.org/chicago

Buddhist Center Colorado Springs
+1 (719) 302 3062
cosprings@diamondway-center.org
www.diamondway.org/cosprings

Buddhist Center Houston
+1 (713) 686 5409
Houston@diamondway-center.org
www.diamondway.org/texas

Buddhist Center La Crosse
+1 (608) 784 1566
Lacrosse@diamondway-center.org
www.diamondway.org/lacrosse

Buddhist Center Los Angeles
+1 (323) 931 1903
LosAngeles@diamondway-center.org
www.diamondway.org/la

Buddhist Center Madison
+1 (608) 251 9175
Madison@diamondway-center.org
www.diamondway.org/madison

Buddhist Group Maui
+1 (808) 283 6849
Maui@diamondway-center.org
www.diamondway.org/maui

Buddhist Center Miami
+1 (305) 756 6921
Miami@diamondway-center.org
www.diamondway.org/miami

Buddhist Center Minneapolis
+1 (612) 825 5055
Minneapolis@diamondway-center.org
www.diamondway.org/minneapolis

Buddhist Center New York
+1 (212) 214 0755
NewYork@diamondway-center.org
www.diamondway.org/ny

Buddhist Group Portland
+1 (503) 281 3631
Portland@diamondway-center.org
www.diamondway.org/portland

Buddhist Center San Diego
+1 (858) 558 0705
SanDiego@diamondway-center.org
www.diamondway.org/sandiego

Buddhist Center San Francisco
+1 (415) 661 6030
SanFrancisco@diamondway-center.org
www.diamondway.org/sf

Buddhist Group Santa Fe
+1 (505) 424 4166
SantaFe@diamondway-center.org

Other Countries

Austria
Buddhist Center Vienna
+43 (1) 2631247
Wien@diamondway-center.org
www.diamantweg.at/wien/

Belgium
Buddhist Center Brussels
+32 (2) 5384800
Brussels@diamondway-center.org
www.bouddhisme-voiedudiamant.be

Czech Republic
Buddhist Center Prague
+420 (608) 866454
Prague@diamondway-center.org
www.bdc.cz/praha

Denmark

Buddhist Center Copenhagen

+45 39292711

Copenhagen@diamondway-center.org

http://www.buddha.dk/buddhistiske_centre/buddhistisk_center
_koebenhavn

Germany

Buddhist Center Berlin Mitte

+49 (30) 24342544

Berlin-Mitte@diamondway-center.org

www.buddhismus-berlin-mitte.de

Buddhist Center Hamburg

+49 (40) 4328380

Hamburg@diamondway-center.org

www.buddhismus-hamburg.de

Buddhist Center Munich

+49 (89) 90547633

Munich@diamondway-center.org

www.buddhismus-münchen.de

Buddhist Europe Center

Buddhismus Siftung Diamantweg

+49 8323 986 8740

info@europe-center.org

www.europe-center.org

Hungary

Buddhist Center Budapest

+36 (1) 3217025

Budapest@diamondway-center.org

Ireland
Buddhist Center Dublin
+353 (1) 8423306
Dublin@diamondway-center.org

Mexico
Buddhist Center Mexico City
+52 (55) 55590629
MexicoCity@diamondway-center.org
www.diamondwaymexico.org

Poland
Buddhist Center Warszawa
+48 (22) 8773408
Warszawa@diamondway-center.org
www.stupahouse.buddyzm.pl

Russia
Buddhist Center St. Petersburg
Petersburg@diamondway-center.org
www.petersburg.buddhism.ru

Spain
Buddhist Retreat Center Karma Gön
+34 (95) 2115197
KarmaGuen@diamondway-center.org
www.karmaguen.org

Switzerland
Buddhist Center Zürich
+41 (0) 44 3820875
Zurich@diamondway-center.org
www.buddhismus.org/zuerich

Venezuela
  Buddhist Center Caracas
  +58 (212) 2849514
  Caracas@diamondway-center.org
  www.budismo-camino-del-diamante.org

For a complete and updated list of Diamond Way Buddhist Centers and more information, please visit:
www.diamondway-buddhism.org

ADDITIONAL PUBLICATIONS

The Great Seal (2004)
Based on an essential Tibetan text written in the 14th century by the third Karmapa, the teachings in this text are designed to give deep insight into the nature of mind.
0-9752954-0-3, Fire Wheel Publishing, USA

Entering the Diamond Way (1999)
The story and spiritual odyssey of Ole and Hannah Nydahl who in 1969 became the first Western students of the great Tibetan master, the 16th Gyalwa Karmapa.
0-931892-03-1, Blue Dolphin Publishing, Inc. California, USA

The Nature of Mind (1993)
In this basic introduction to Buddhism, Lama Ole offers a way to integrate compassion and wisdom in daily life.
0-931892-58-9, Blue Dolphin Publishing, Inc. California, USA

Riding the Tiger (1992)
The inside story of the development of Tibetan Buddhism in the West.
0-931892-67-8, Blue Dolphin Publishing, Inc. California, USA

Mahamudra (1990)
A commentary on the 14th century wishing prayer for the attainment of ultimate insight into the nature of reality. This Mahamudra prayer was composed by the third Karmapa, Rangjung Dorje.
0-931892-69-4, Blue Dolphin Publishing, Inc. California, USA

Ngondro (1990)

Ngondro means *something which precedes* and are the preliminary practices in Tibetan Buddhism. In a direct and very practical way, Lama Ole explains these methods that help to purify negativity and to accumulate merit and wisdom.

0-931892-23-6, Blue Dolphin Publishing, Inc. California, USA

ENDNOTES

[1] Walter Evans-Wentz, *Tibet's Great Yogi Milarepa: A Biography from the Tibetan* (Oxford University Press, 2000).

[2] Keith Dowman (trans.), *The Divine Madman: The sublime life and songs of Drukpa Kunley* (Rider, 1980).

[3] *The Jewel Ornament of Liberation: The Wish-fulfilling Gem of the Noble Teachings* by Gampopa (Snow Lion Publications, 1998)

[4] Lama Ole Nydahl, *The Great Seal: The Mahamudra View of Diamond Way Buddhism* (San Francisco: Fire Wheel Publishing, 2004).

BOOKS

O is a symbol of the world, of oneness and unity. In different cultures it also means the "eye," symbolizing knowledge and insight. We aim to publish books that are accessible, constructive and that challenge accepted opinion, both that of academia and the "moral majority."

Our books are available in all good English language bookstores worldwide. If you don't see the book on the shelves ask the bookstore to order it for you, quoting the ISBN number and title. Alternatively you can order online (all major online retail sites carry our titles) or contact the distributor in the relevant country, listed on the copyright page.

See our website www.o-books.net for a full list of over 500 titles, growing by 100 a year.

And tune in to myspiritradio.com for our book review radio show, hosted by June-Elleni Laine, where you can listen to the authors discussing their books.

MySpiritRadio

SOME RECENT O BOOKS

Everyday Buddha
Lawrence Ellyard

Whether you already have a copy of the Dhammapada or not, I recommend you get this. If you are new to Buddhism this is a great place to start. The whole feel of the book is lovely, the layout of the verses is clear and the simple illustrations are very beautiful, catching a feel for the original work. His Holiness the Dalai Lama's foreword is particularly beautiful, worth the purchase price alone. Lawrence's introduction is clear and simple and sets the context for what follows without getting bogged down in information... I congradulate all involved in this project and have put the book on my recommended list.
Nova Magazine

1905047304   144pp **£9.99 $19.95**

The Other Buddhism
Amida Comes West
Caroline Brazier

An essential book for Buddhists, for students of religion, and for therapists of all schools, and for anyone who seeks an improved ability to cope with the stresses of our everyday world.
Jim Pym, editor of *Pure Land Notes*

978-1-84694-0   304pp **£11.99 $24.95**

Who Loves Dies Well
On the Brink of Buddha's Pure Land
David Brazier

Practical, moving and full of deep love for the reader, and as such is the perfect guide to newcomers and experienced Buddhists alike. **Jim Pym**, author of *You Don't Have to Sit on the Floor.*

9781846940453 256pp **£11.99 $19.95**

A Global Guide to Interfaith
Reflections From Around the World
Sandy Bharat

This amazing book gives a wonderful picture of the variety and excitement of this journey of discovery.
Rev Dr. Marcus Braybrooke, President of the World Congress of Faiths

1905047975   336pp **£19.99 $34.95**

Living With Honour
A Pagan Ethics
Emma Restall Orr

This is an excellent pioneering work, erudite, courageous and imaginative, that provides a new kind of ethics, linked to a newly appeared complex of religions, which are founded on some very old human truths.
Professor Ronald Hutton, world expert on paganism and author of *The Triumph of the Moon*

9781846940941   368pp **£11.99 $24.95**

Peace Prayers
From the World's Faiths
Roger Grainger

Deeply humbling. This is a precious little book for those interested in building bridges and doing something practical about peace. **Odyssey**

1905047665   144pp **£11.99 $19.95**

Shamanic Reiki
Expanded Ways of Workling with Universal Life Force Energy
Llyn Roberts and Robert Levy

The alchemy of shamanism and Reiki is nothing less than pure gold in the hands of Llyn Roberts and Robert Levy. Shamanic Reiki brings the concept of energy healing to a whole new level. More than a how-to-book, it speaks to the health of the human spirit, a journey we must all complete.
Brian Luke Seaward, Ph.D., author of *Stand Like Mountain, Flow Like Water, Quiet Mind, Fearless Heart*

9781846940378   208pp **£9.99 $19.95**

The Good Remembering
A Message for our Times
Llyn Roberts

Llyn's work changed my life. "The Good Remembering" is the most important book I've ever read.
John Perkins, *NY Times* best selling author of *Confessions of an Economic Hit Man*

1846940389   96pp **£7.99 $16.95**

The Last of the Shor Shamans
Alexander and Luba Arbachakov

The publication of Alexander and Luba Arbachakov's 2004 study of Shamanism in their own community in Siberia is an important addition to the study of the anthropology and sociology of the peoples of Russia. Joanna Dobson's excellent English translation of the Arbachakov's work brings to a wider international audience a fascinating glimpse into the rapidly disappearing traditional world of the Shor Mountain people. That the few and very elderly Shortsi Shamans were willing to share their beliefs and experiences with the Arbachakov's has enabled us all to peer into this mysterious and mystic world. **Frederick Lundahl**, retired American Diplomat and specialist on Central Asia

9781846941276   96pp **£9.99 $19.95**

The Thoughtful Guide to Religion
Why it began, how it works, and where it's going
Ivor Morrish

A massive amount of material, clearly written, readable and never dry. the fruit of a lifetime's study, a splendid book. It is a major achievement to cover so much background in a volume compact enough to read on the bus. Morris is particularly good on illustrating the inter-relationships betwen religions. I found it hard to put down.
Faith and Freedom

190504769X   384pp £24.99 $34.95

The House of Wisdom
Yoga of the East and West
Swami Dharmananda Saraswati and Santoshan

Swamiji has shared her wisdom with her students for many years. Now her profound and enlightening writings, and those of Santoshan, are made available to a wider audience in this excellent book. The House of Wisdom *is a real treasure-house of spiritual knowledge.*
Priya Shakti (Julie Friedeberger), author of *The Healing Power of Yoga*

1846940249   224pp **£11.99 $22.95**

Sivananda Buried Yoga
Yogi Manmoyanand

Panning the one-dimensional keep-fit view of yoga in the west and advocating a return to the depth and breadth of yoga's true roots, yogi manmoyanand's controversial new book exceeded all expectations and became an instant bestseller – not only at Watkins, but across the globe.
Watkins Books, London

978-1-84694-151-1   320pp **£9.99 $19.95**

Who on EARTH was JESUS?
the modern quest for the Jesus of history
David Boulton

What happens when the Christ of faith meets the Jesus of history? This is the question that preoccupies Boulton in an amazingly good synthesis of historical Jesus scholarship. His scope is as wide-ranging as it is even-handed; from theologians to scholars to popes, he distills their thoughts into a comprehensible and

comprehensive survey of the best of the contemporary thinkers. Readers will find no overt proselytizing in this book. Instead, the author treats them to an unbiased look at the ever-changing discipline of Jesus studies. In the end, Boulton understands that it is not the scholar, nor the theologian, who will define the kingdom on Earth. Rather, it will be the job of all of us to discern the Jesus of today from words written long ago. This book is not to be missed.
Publisher's Weekly

9781846940187   448pp **£14.99 $29.95**

Who Is Right About God?
Thinking Through Christian Attitudes in a World of Many Faiths
Duncan Raynor

This book is both important and readable, because it has been forged in the daily "real time" interplay between the issues and views that it discusses, and because it is given rigour and intellectual coherence by the gifted author, who has an Oxford training in philosophy, as well as theology.
The Very Revd Robert Grimley, Dean of Bristol Cathedral

9781846941030   144pp **£11.99 $24.95**